OPA WAXES PROPHETIC

OPA WAXES PROPHETIC

Iconoclasts who became Icons

By

C.O. Stephens

Opa Waxes Prophetic
Publication © 2020 Mbokodo Publishers
Text © 2020 CO Stephens
ISBN-13: 978-1-990919-11-4 (Paperback)
ISBN-13: 978-1-990919-12-1 (PDF)
ISBN-13: 978-1-990919-13-8 (eBook)[1]
Publisher: M.R. Mbokodo
Proofreading: CO Stephens
Cover Design: M.R. Mbokodo
Photo Credit:
Published by

Typeset in 10/12 Adobe Garamond Pro by Mbokodo Publishers
Printed by Mbokodo Publishers 1 2 3 4 5 1 2

---

1.   http://www.mbokodopublishers.eshop.co.za/

mbokodopublishers@gmail.com
Every effort has been made to obtain copyright permission for the material used in this book. Please contact the Author with any queries in this regard

DEFINITION OF TERMS

Acronym	Definition
AD	Anno Domini
AIC	Africa-Initiated Churches
AIDS	Acquired Immune Deficiency Syndrome
AU	African Union
CCF	Co-operative Commonwealth Federation
CSO	Civil Society Organisation
C4L	Desmond Tutu Centre for Leadership
EFF	Economic Freedom Fighters
HIV	Human Immunodeficiency Virus
ICT	Information and Communications Technology
LMS	London Missionary Society
MOU	Memorandum of Understanding
MP	Member of Parliament
NGO	Non-Government Organisation
OAU	Organization of African Unity
OT	Old Testament
OVC	Orphans and Vulnerable Children
SACC	South African Council of Churches
UK	United Kingdom
USA	United States of America
ZCC	Zion Christian Church

Page   ICONIC

Page   ICONIC

PREAMBLE

RE-CYCLING is a virtue and these re-cycled portraits are all iconic. Through them, at different times over the decades, readers were able to see deeper Truth.

History is like that – it tells stories of the past that bear relevance on the present. Surely this is why the Old Testament is so often quoted in the New Testament? That is why we keep records. Not just for posterity but to guide us into the future.

Speaking of the Old Testament, it has four parts:

1. Books of Law
2. Books of History
3. Books of Literature
4. Books of Prophecy

From this I deduce that both recording history and speaking truth to power prophetically are important aspects of life in community. As are the arts – the psalms of worships, poems, songs, laments and romances.

Foundational to all of these is the Law or the constitutional framework that binds citizens together. For "lawlessness" is the enemy of civilization and culture.

When it comes to speaking truth to power, names like Nathan and Amos come to mind. Nathan confronted the king, Amos confronted the people. We need to do both.

Our role – in the memorable words of Dorothy Day - is to comfort the afflicted... *and to afflict the comfortable.*

<u>Methodology</u>

This book is a collection. It is composed of different portraits that have been painted of different activists worthy of being our role-models. It has been written from time to time over a long period of years. So it is a kind of re-cycling or anthology.

The sense was that by gathering these all into one volume, one could see a "host of witnesses" and get some synergy from "the communion of saints". However, there is no "plot" to this book, which might make it seem a bit incoherent. Remember that this is the twin to another collection – of my poems. Forty poems written over fifty years, so each one is a stand-alone. So it is with these icons, and these are also very subjective, like poems are. So there is not a high level of objectivity.

Instead, the structure of the book is simply the chronology of the role-models. So the earliest iconoclasts appear first. This made it possible to batch them into chapters, not just a string of single portraits, perhaps in alphabetical order. Or it could have been from the longest portrait to the shortest? But each and every one of them speaks to the present not to the past.

The word "sin" is used 930 times in the Bible. The word "justice" is used 2000 times. What does this tell you? Could it be more spiritual to focus on justice than on sin?

Another thing to bear in mind is that we in English translate the Hebrew word for "justice" into two words – "justice" sometimes and "righteousness" other times. This does not happen in other languages, for example in Portuguese where only one word is always used – "*justica*". Perhaps English is richer in this respect? Just like the Inuit, in Canada, who have five words for "snow". All those Inuit words were never needed in the relatively green and warm British Isles, where English arose (first as a creole of other European languages and eventually as a language in its own right).

Could this splitting the translation of "justice" into two words have the collateral effect that we don't see its relative predominance? Listen to the two sample verses that follow. They would seem somehow diminished by using one and the same word. But when no distinction is made between the two semantic ranges, ever, then we would recognize how much more this key word is repeated.

Isaiah 1: 17 - *Learn to do good; Seek justice, Reprove the ruthless, Defend the orphan, Plead for the wisdom.*

Proverbs 21: 21 - *Whoever pursues righteousness and love finds life, prosperity and honour.*

Some might see righteousness as the opposite of sinfulness? If by righteousness what we really mean is "justice", that nuance might help us to understand the need for more activism and less pietism? (Although iconic pietists like Auguste Frank and George Muller were among the greatest activists ever, in their own way, and for their own time.)

A Patch-work Quilt

Most readers will be familiar with this kind of blanket – made from recycled cut-offs from other sewing projects. It is not only a way to economize - the quilts do have their own design as well. On the square blanket may be a circle, with a star inside the circle. Thus the patch-work quilt is not made from just randomly sewing pieces together, it does has a motif of its own.

Between the covers of this book are some "floating" gems that dress up the design. But the collection does have its own shape and purpose – to inspire people to *speak truth to power*.

In today's trending for flat management structures we occasionally speak of Bishops, but mostly of Ministers, Pastors or Preachers. We sometimes hear of an Evangelist, but we rarely hear of Prophets. That is not true of the Africa Initiated Churches. I have sat in a room with a Prophet at Moria. No chairs or tables, certainly no couches like a psychiatrist uses. You sit on the mat or kneel to pray. The prophet lies down on the same mat and listens. My personal experience is that what a Prophet has to say is worth listening to. S/he has *insight*. It is not "process intervention" like a Counselor might use. It is "content intervention" because s/he has a spiritual gift, honed by experience. S/he speaks with deep perception.

Perhaps this is the big message of this collection of writings? Acts 2 make it clear that the great mark of the New Covenant is prophecy, and not by special people but by "sons and daughters" and "handmaids and servants". St. Paul is quite clear in I Corinthians 14:29-31 – we may ALL prophecy!!

And prophecy is for the present – not the future. So many speakers or writers on Prophecy tell us what God is going to do down the track. God is not on holidays – he will give us instructions for today's challenges. Listen to the voice crying in the veld. Move over Bishops, Pastors and Evangelists, and make room for Prophets. *"Prepare ye the way of the Lord"*.

But readers beware! While the structure of the book follows a familiar pathway, from Old Testament to New Testament to church history – that *is not what I am writing about*. It's almost like not being able to watch a 3D movie without wearing the right lenses. My message – the prophecy – comes in glimpses gleaned when these iconic iconoclasts are interpreted *for the present*.

Iconic and Iconoclast

This play on words (iconic and iconoclast) is very useful. In the Eastern Orthodox church and theology, icons are something akin to the stained-glass windows of Western Europe. They are not idols, but images through which the real Truth can be perceived.

This anthology collects several dozen iconoclasts ("those who destroy cherished customs") from over four millennia. But it does much more than that – it uses them to help us see the Truth about today's ministry in general and activism in particular. If our "gaps" can be illuminated and thus the impact of overall ministry strengthened, then the book was worth writing, and will be worth reading too.

If there is a person or even a period that is passed by, that is not significant. This is only an anthology of what I have previously written about, to cajole and inspire my readers. The collection does not claim to be comprehensive, but is just a sampling. Some portraits are short and some are long – that signifies nothing about their value.

Speaking personally, Martin Luther is probably my greatest hero? But he gets only one page. Whereas the mother of South Africa, Krotoa, gets several pages. She probably deserves more, but she did not have the impact on history that Luther had. So what? All we have here are the "greatest hits" from my previous efforts to promote activism at one point or another of my career. There are no "major prophets" and "minor prophets" – all the portraits of iconoclasts contribute to the collage. They might have been tweaked ever so slightly but they are substantially as they originally appeared.

Watch how I do it

Before looking at the individual portraits of ad hoc role-models, remember that this is an anthology to explore and interpret *their relevance* to diverse events in my lifetime - that emerged over a period of years, even decades. This is the book's usefulness – to show that prophetic ministry is about *insight* more than *foresight*. It is about interpreting the *present* more than foretelling the *future*.

More of us in ministry need to do this more.

So don't mind the jostling from one historical era to another or from one "present" to another as the portraits were not written in sequence. Rather watch closely how much one icon of the past can inform the present. I hope that all readers will enjoy the travelogue, and that some readers will go on to practice this same kind of iconography in their own ministry.

Bear in mind that the chronology is of the portraits. But I did not write them in that order, so the practical applications (i.e the "significance") do jump around a bit. It's like the New Testament – where the epistles of St Paul are placed from the longest one down to the shortest. Even though he wrote some of the shorter ones earlier! For example, his epistle to the Galatians is a short synopsis of what he later wrote to the Romans. But the <u>Book of Romans</u> appears first in the table of contents. Don't let this jostling confuse you. Focus on the portraits of the iconoclasts and scan them for Truth.

The structure is just there so that the patches can be sewn together in a unique design.

An Iconography

The Tate Gallery website defines an iconography as "a particular range or system of types of image used by an artist or artists to convey particular meanings".

Perhaps a simpler definition of iconography is "the containment of deeper meanings in simple representations. It often makes use of symbolism to generate narrative".

It is actually a bit like Expository Preaching, because there are two elements – meaning and significance. When a minister preaches his way through a chapter or even a book of the Bible, he first has to unpack what it is saying. Then he needs to apply that in a probing and relevant way to his listeners. Sometimes preachers are really good at conveying their detailed research into the meaning. Perhaps they are relatively timid to apply it to a congregation of people much like themselves? What that amounts to is taking the sword of the Lord out of its scabbard, and flailing it around in the air, where people can see it gleaming and shining. But a sword exists for a purpose. The sword of the Lord is sharp enough to cut spirit from soul. It can slice through attitudes and lop off bad habits.

From earliest times Christian iconography has been a symbolic code, showing the faithful one thing and inviting them to see *in it* the figure of another. Usually this is done in art, but in this book it is in narrative. Parables are a great example – they tell a story, which is easy to remember. Then you "get it" in terms of the deeper message. This book is about the significance, not about the portraits. There is a danger, in fact, that we cherish the icon or stained glass window more than the message. Then these become more of an idol than an icon. So keep your eye on *the relevance*.

1. PATRIARCHS AND PROPHETS

Noah, Ham and Cush

After the flood, God pushed the reset button with Noah's family. Noah had three sons – Shem, Ham and Japeth. Noah's son Ham had five sons, one of whom was Cush, the father of Nimrod (and others). Nimrod became the first "king" of this area that we call Mesopotamia, from Persia to Egypt. He ruled an area called Shinar - from Ur of the Chaldees up to Assyria – taking in Babylon.

One of Shem's sons was Arphaxad, one of the forefathers of Serud, father of Nahor, father of Terah, father of Abraham. Abraham was the oldest of three sons, his two younger brothers were Haran and Nahor II. Terah accompanied Abraham, who decided to leave Ur of the Chaldees and head up-river to higher ground, and to higher moral ground.

Nimrod was human but came to be revered as a god, because of his prowess as a hunter and a conqueror. Some people believe that Abraham's departure from the Chaldean city of Ur – eventually to the Levant – was a result of his disapproval of Noah's great-grandson Nimrod. There are some extra-biblical accounts of Abraham encountering Nimrod to register his disapproval. That people were now turning from the worship of God to worshipping a man.

One manifestation of this problem in our time is when demagogues capture the State. Abraham's challenge to Nimrod could be summed up by the words of a speech given by Shamila Batohi, the new National Director of Public Prosecutions in South Africa. She said: "*We have a very small window of opportunity to turn the situation around.*" South Africa needs a reminder that the calamities and challenges being experienced did not emerge in isolation. There is always a cosmic struggle going on behind these events. Shamila Batohi is merely one of the actors at the human level. In her speech, she said: *"Corruption has become so widespread that there is a real danger of it becoming entrenched and normalised in South Africa unless something serious happens soon. For too long, corrupt politicians, government employees and business leaders have acted almost with impunity to plunder the scarce resources of our country."* It is naïve to think that the criminal syndicates that have tried to overthrow South Africa's democratic equilibrium are acting in isolation.

Somehow, rebellion against God (i.e. against monotheism) always smacks of Nimrod, the great-grandson of Noah. He should have known better! Mesopotamia became a very wicked place – as well as a very powerful place – only a few generations after God sent the flood to punish all the wickedness that had preceded it. Building the tower of Babel (from which Babylon takes its name) may have been just an innocuous ziggurat? Or was it - cosmically - a symbol of rebellion?

In Genesis 10: 11-12 it says: *"And Cush was the father of Nimrod, who began to be a mighty one on the earth. He was a mighty hunter before the LORD; so it is said, "Like Nimrod, a mighty hunter before the LORD." His kingdom began in Babylon, Erech, Accad, and Calneh, in the land of Shinar. From that land he went forth into Assyria, where he built Nineveh, Rehoboth-Ir, Calah, and Resen, which is between Nineveh and the great city of Calah."*

One variation of Nimrod's bio says that as a great-grandson of Noah he did know better, so he fled to Assyria (like Abraham did too - on his way to the Levant). Where God rewarded Nimrod - for sticking with monotheism. He thus became the first to rule as a "king" after the flood. He even coined the word "crown"! In fact, Nimrod was the first to ever wear one. Perhaps it was after this that he lost his way? (For power corrupts, and absolute power corrupts absolutely.)

Another reason that he moved to Assyria could have been because of the way God confounded the defiant people of Babylon with 72 different languages? At any rate Nimrod had two sons – Bendeuci and Eliezar. Somehow, the younger son Eliezar became the mordomo of Abraham, basically the manager of his household. Eliezar is the one who Abraham sent to Ur to find a suitable wife for his son, in an arranged marriage. He returned with Rebekah, who was in fact Isaac's distant relative, daughter of Bethuel. Abraham's father Terah and Nahor were brothers. Bethuel was one of Nahor's son. So Isaac's marriage to Rebekah was inter-generational (as well as sight-unseen).

Whether monotheism relapsed into polytheism under Nimrod or in the cities that he fled to Assyria from, Mesopotamia slipped back into apostasy. One of its major centres of polytheism was Calah. The Bible is clear that monotheism preceded polytheism everywhere, not the other way around. Starting first in the Garden of Eden, and then again after the flood. Apostate polytheism was developed by Cush and his wife Semiramis and later propagated by their son Nimrod. It infected every city and there will be great rejoicing when it is pulled down (Revelation 18).

According to Kang and Wilson, the Chinese left Mesopotamia around 2200 BC (just after the confounding of languages at Babylon). They lived in isolation and were known as "the One God people" until the fifth century BC when Confucius and Taoism arrived on the scene. Genesis is clearly seen in the original Chinese script. For example, the symbol for the Holy Spirit is derived from Genesis 1:2:

| heaven | cover | water | rain | three person | worker of magic | Spirit |

Spirit

Genesis 1 is not a fairy story. It is evidenced in the history of every nation and confirmed by the apostate adaption of early happenings by the architects of rebellion. That is the Biblical perspective anyway.

There are almost 11 chapters before Abraham is mentioned, including the account of Noah and the flood. The primordial relationship between God and humans keeps getting interrupted.

In his seminal thinking on pre-history of southern Africa, Michael Tellinger sees evidence of a flood right across the African sub-continent. Although some believe that the flood of Noah was a regional flood in Mesopotamia. What a shame that in such a short time, apostasy set in again, in the form of polytheism. It makes me think of that famous book by Malcolm Muggeridge – <u>Jesus Rediscovered</u>. You can lose your way in this mall of religions and ideologies, and turn from the one true God. But then he comes looking for you like a lost sheep. So you rediscover Him.

<u>In Praise of Monotheism</u>

As a lover of history, I have been reading the biography of a pioneer missionary in South Africa. He is the one who first carried the good news (i.e. the "gospel" in Old English) to the indigenous Bantu tribes in southern Africa. This led me to read of a Xhosa advisor to King Gaika, named Ntsikana. He first heard about the white man's God from this Dutch missionary. Johannes van der Kemp only planted the seed in Ntsikana's heart and mind. But over a decade later, Ntsikana abandoned his old gods and converted to Christianity.

In Gaika's kraal, Ntsikana was a poet as well as a senior advisor. He wrote many battle hymns for the Xhosa warriors. He later applied these talents to writing hymns for Christian worship. For example, the Great Hymn <u>Ulo Tixo 'Mkulu</u>:

Those hands of thine, they are wounded
Those feet of thine, they are wounded
Thy blood, why is it streaming?
Thy blood, it was shed for me

What did it take to convince one poet, songwriter and royal advisor to convert to monotheism? This question took me back in my thinking to Mohamed, who converted Saudi Arabia to monotheism.

Until he converted its tribes to Islam, that whole peninsula had remained polytheist. It was not an easy task! Before long, though, that religion spread across North Africa too, and penetrated into western Europe through Spain as well as eastern Europe from the Ottoman Empire.

Mohamed was familiar with both Christianity and Judaism. Both are monotheist, and of course Christianity had its roots in Judaism. Islam regards both Jesus and Moses as among its greatest prophets. Moses was a great African leader, predating Ntsikana by 3300 years. Of Jewish birth, he was raised in an Egyptian home, which was polytheist like most of Africa was at that time. But as he grew older, he returned to the monotheist faith of his mother, who called Abraham her "father". Out of this exposure to both African polytheism and Judaism, Moses consolidated his true people into a nation. He combined the education that he was blessed with by the African pharaoh who adopted him, with the learning that he received from his Jewish mother (who the royal family had found and hired to be her own son's Nanny).

Speaking of education, Israel was the first country to become fully literate – that is 98 percent. This included women and slaves, because the Jews wanted everyone to read the Law of Moses themselves. By 500 BC, all citizens in Israel could read and write. The next nation to reach this threshold was England - in 1898. The USA followed about 1920. One of the great feats of the Russian revolution was bringing it up to this threshold of functional literacy in about 25 years – by the 1930s. South Africa is not there yet – it reached 93 percent in 2015.

Father Abraham left Ur of the Chaldees in around 1900 BC. (Ntsikana met Johannes van der kemp around 1800 AD.) Mesopotamia had relapsed into polytheism, and Abraham departed to follow monotheism, on the western frontier. From Israel, Abraham later sent Eliezer back to Ur to find a wife for his son Isaac. He found Rebekah and negotiated the Lobola for her.

But Abraham was not the original monotheist. Biblically, humans were monotheist from the Garden of Eden. But they lost their way, so God sent the flood. Noah started with a "remnant" of God's people. But they fell into apostasy and polytheism again.

One of those who rediscovered monotheism was Zoroaster (a k a Zarathustra), in Persia. He evangelized Persia (now Iran) and replaced its polytheism with the worship of one God. That is, until it was converted to Islam, some 3000 later. Zoroastrianism remained the predominant religion of Persia while cities like Ur of the Chaldees and Babylon rose - not far from the Iranian border. Zoroastrianism could well have been known to Abraham, and influential in his decision to leave Ur and polytheism behind? Persia may have converted from Zoroastrianism to Islam, but it stuck with monotheism! Islam regards Zoroaster as one of its prophets.

Ethiopia converted to Judaism about 1000 BC at the time of Solomon, and later to Christianity, so monotheism was known to Africa long before Ntsikana's conversion.

The Greek mathematician Pythagoras was educated in Babylon. While there, he learned of Zoroaster's system of religious ethics called Masdayasna (i.e. worship of wisdom). By translating this he coined a new word in Greek – "philosophy".

Humanism was the world's first secular religion. It seeks to replace human accountability to God with a system of "human rights", making us accountable to one another. This started at the time of the Protestant Reformation around 500 years ago. In fact, one of the early Humanists was Erasmus, whose writings really inspired Martin Luther. But three strands of humanism have emerged. First there is liberal humanism, which sanctifies humans. Its belief in the free and sacred nature of the individual is descended from the Christian belief in free and individual souls.

Second there is socialist humanism. It has a different understanding of "humanity" – that it is collective rather than individualistic. This is also built on monotheistic foundations. The notion of equality is a revamped version of the monotheistic belief that all souls are equal before God.

Third, there is evolutionary humanism, which mixes it with strong doses of Darwinism. Unlike other humanists, this strand regards humanity - not something universal or eternal - but instead a mutable species that can improve or degenerate. But all three strands want to turn us away from God.

Missionaries like van der Kemp preached monotheism to converts like Ntsikana, trying to turn them back to God. Africa became deeply Christianized, and also, since then, Christianity has become deeply Africanized. I have a concern – about Humanism's agenda – if its ultimate goal is to replace monotheism. While traditional and religious rights are entrenched in the Constitution, it is fundamentally a rights-based document. This is moving South Africa out of its comfort zone, into a secular space. Even when most citizens are deeply religious. This worries me.

Monotheism has prevailed for thousands of years, albeit in different manifestations. Are we ready to let that go for a new secular religion that is only a few centuries old? (Marxism is even younger, not even two centuries old.) Aboriginal beliefs go back into pre-history. But I am inclined to keep monotheism as a rudder under the good ship *Rainbow*. Blessed is the nation whose God is the Lord.

Thank God for Ntsikana, for his wisdom, humility and peace-loving posture. Like Zoroaster, Abraham, Moses and Mohamed, he cajoled his own people to convert to monotheism. South Africa is not yet ready to let it go. I hope the day will never come that humanity sanctifies itself.

Job – A Window on Monotheism

According to Zoroastrian dualism, the world is created by two opposing forces. The *good* deity Ahura Mazda created everything good, but for everything good that was created, Angra Mainyu created an evil counterpart. This resulted in the existence of the Daeva or six archdemons – who command a countless numbers of demons. These archdemons stay in exact opposition to the Amesha Spenta, a class of six divine entities emanating from the wise lord Ahura Mazda. Maybe we now call them archangels? Just as most stories have a hero and a villain, there is always this tension in life. Sometimes the cosmic beings encounter humans directly – sort of like meeting extra terrestrials. But usually they use evil humans or villains as "fronting". These are the protagonists that we usually encounter, while our angels or archangels do battle with their counterparts on our behalf.

One of the greatest works of literature is also one of the greatest poems in human history – <u>The Book of Job</u>. It has dual prologues. Instead of the way the Brothers Grimm started stories with "Once upon a time", you basically get "Twice upon a time" – two preambles to the same biography. One is the human story narrative, Job's success and good fortune - until he slams into calamity and his health collapses. The other prologue is about God meeting the Devil in the court of heaven. They actually talk about Job. So there is a dualism that runs through the book – human narrative level and cosmic insight level.

The predominant religion of ancient Persia was Zoroastrianism. Dating the life of its great prophet Zoroaster is difficult - estimates vary. But it was he who entrenched "ethical dualism" in people's thinking before the Axial Age. He perceived a cosmic clash between Good and Evil, each with its ultimate destination (heaven and hell). He perceived that individuals are accountable and that one day there will be a Judgment. He was able to rediscover monotheism from a context of rampant polytheism. Meanwhile, the apostasy of polytheism thrived in Egypt, the Middle East and Europe (e.g. Greece and Rome were polytheistic until challenged by the monotheism of Christianity, centuries later).

The two prologues to Job illustrate this dualism, which was expressed much later by St Paul: "For we wrestle not against flesh and blood, but against principalities and powers, against the rulers of the darkness of this world." Judaism and Christianity both arose from the Middle East. So did Islam. In fact, the Koran mentions 25 prophets, among them are Zarathustra, Job and Abraham.

History repeats itself. Time is of the essence. We do not just struggle against the prospect of a Mafia State - entrenched gangsterism in the form of criminal syndicates calling the shots. The big picture is that there is an on-going cosmic battle between Good and Evil. It has Zoroastrian proportions. Remember the lessons of Noah, Job and Abraham. All monotheists revere these three figures. So the struggle has Biblical proportions as well. Let us reject apostasy and revisit the faith of our ancestors.

It is interesting to note that Saudi Arabia was not much affected by all this ancient history. Until the rise of Islam brought it to the fore as a regional power. That is certainly still playing out in the Middle East. One of Mohammed's great accomplishments was to replace the polytheism of Saudi Arabia with Islam – in his time. When you think that only one Pharaoh in Egypt ever tried to do so, and did not succeed because of the vested interests of polytheism, this was no mean accomplishment. It is not an easy thing to "rediscover monotheism", but God is always seeking to reconnect with those who have wandered into other beliefs or ideologies.

Only one Egyptian pharaoh - Akhenaten – ever tried to convert his culture from polytheism. This was in about 1350 BC, but his "rediscovery of monotheism" was not widely accepted. After his death, his monuments were dismantled and hidden, statues of him were destroyed, and his name was struck from the roll of king. Polytheism was gradually restored, and about twelve years after his death, when rulers without clear rights of succession from the 18th Dynasty founded a new dynasty, they discredited Akhenaten and his immediate successors, referring to Akhenaten himself as "the enemy" or "that criminal" in archival records. Make no mistake that the enemies of monotheism will be friendly or even tolerant.

How much time is left before the vested interests of Humanism and Marxism crowd out any prospect of the pendulum swinging back to monotheism? Is this bringing us closer to the Judgment Day? When the sheep will be separated from the goats.

Abraham versus Nimrod

There are two versions to the narrative, around the time when Abraham decided to emigrate from Ur. One is that Nimrod ordered his subjects to fetch firewood for four years so he could build the biggest fire ever seen, in which to burn Abraham. (This would be the Ace Magashule version.)

The other version is that Nimrod repented, and gave his son Eliezer to Abraham as a majordomo. Included in Eliezar's roles of managing Abraham's household was negotiating the Lobola for Rebekah. (This would be the Pravin Gordhan version of the narrative.)

We can see a kind of dualism in current event around us. For example, when ex-President Zuma testified at the Zondo Commission; or when Ace Magashule took on Derrick Hanekom; or in the clash between Pravin Gordhan and the Public Protector. These are more than just politics. The ruling party taking on a foundation started by one of its own illustrious Treason Trialists is another clue. Just as cosmic forces came down on Job like a ton of bricks, South Africa has been put through the ringer. God is allowing it for a reason.

Will a Humanist Constitution with a man-centred Bill of Rights hold? Or is it time to refresh our roots of monotheism – in Christianity, Islam and Judaism? Even for the polytheists, losing bazillions of Rand to plunderers of the public purse must be unacceptable, although without the "In God We Trust" as their credo, do either polytheists or humanists ultimately have any absolutes? As Relativism takes over, the criminal justice system is set adrift. If there is ultimately no right or wrong, how enforceable do laws become, and how long will it be before South Africa ends up a mafia state?

The philosopher Voltaire stated that if God did not exist, it would be necessary to invent Him.

Melchizadek, Jesse and Balaam

Zoroastrian faith was firmly entrenched in ancient Persia long before Abraham emigrated from Ur of the Chaldees. But as Abraham and his descendents moved around the Levant, they did encounter other pockets of monotheism. For example, when Abraham first arrived at Salem (the site of Jerusalem) he found a priest/king already there called Melchizadek, who was a monotheist. Some analysts believe that Melchizedek (= the king of righteousness) was really Shem - because Abraham tithed to him. Or one of his descendants.

Some also think that Melchizedek was the Egyptian Hercules, the one who is portrayed with the horn in his mouth that prosecuted Nimrod in the court of Egypt? In these generations after the flood, polytheism spread out and so many myths and legends are re-told in different pantheons with local names. Even though they are referring to the same primordial narratives. Zoroaster reclaimed Persia from polytheism, but it could not be suppressed in Egypt due to the vested interests of polytheism. From there is spread to Greece and thence to Rome. Saudi Arabia also slipped back into polytheism until the time of Mohammed. Meanwhile Christianity broke out in Egypt, and then later Islam.

Similarly, in 2020, the Covid-19 pandemic spread out from one origin. We don't yet know who "Patient Zero" is by name, but we do know that the epicentre of the pandemic moved from China to Europe then on to America. Until there is a vaccine available, there could be on-going episodes of "the hammer and the dance". This is exactly how apostasy spread out after the flood, from Cush to Nimrod and beyond, as Nimrod travelled far and wide as a military conqueror, and esteemed as a god.

I can see Abraham migrating away from polytheism with a cloth mask over his face! He didn't want to catch that apostasy. And as he moved around the Levant, he found a few others – here and there - wearing masks as well. They were the die-hard monotheists.

Centuries later when Moses escaped from Egypt for killing a soldier in the forces that were oppressing his people, he encountered Jesse – another monotheist. And before long, as Joshua marched out of the desert to claim the Promised Land, he met a prophet name Balaam, who was also a monotheist - with a talking donkey.

Zoroaster rediscovered monotheism in Persia, Constantine rediscovered it in Europe, and Mohammed rediscovered it in Saudi Arabia. These are not to be confused with Melchizedek, Job, Abraham, Jesse and Balaam – who are in a line of Noah's descendants who kept the faith. Others came back to it, but these never left the worship of the one true God.

These icons constitute a challenge to the faiths of monotheism to join the impetus to defeat corruption, patronage and above all State Capture. We can thank a Dominican priest Father Mayibe for filing the first complaint about State Capture with the Public Protector. We can also thank the Methodist Church's "Unburdening Panel" for its analysis and insights into State Capture.

But more than any others in Civil Society, we monotheists are the ones who can perceive the ethical dualism behind the near and present danger. Together we share a psalm vision that talks about "leading captivity captive". We firmly believe that good will always triumph over evil.

Jacob - Social Distancing in 1746 B.C.

"And he set a distance of three days' journey between himself and Jacob, and Jacob pastured the rest of Laban's flock." This happened in what is now Syria, in Genesis 30:36. It was intentional and it was to control the spread of something un-desired.

Laban was the brother of Abraham. Both had left Ur and headed upstream. Laban settled in Syria but Abraham later migrated again, further south into what is now Israel.

Laban's nephew Jacob was not selling "snake-oil" when he went to his uncle with an offer. He had been tricked by Laban into working seven years to pay for his bride, only to get delivery of the bride's sister. So he had to work another period for his cherished bride. That's the background of polygamy, Jacob married two sisters. During this period, Jacob was evidently educating himself. For his proposal was well-researched and Laban swallowed the bait – hook, line and sinker.

Jacob basically said, You don't have to pay me, I will manage your flocks. All I ask in return is that you give me all the sheep and goats that are not one-colour. These are normally few, and the grade of wool and hide is lower, so Laban thought that he had got the better end of the new deal with Jacob.

But Jacob insisted on social distancing – he would pasture his flocks and pitch his tents at a three days' journey from Laban. This is what played out, but Jacob had become something of a geneticist. Probably by close observation of "herd health" while he was working for Uncle Laban as a rancher.

For one thing, in spite of the distance between them, their herds would be distinct. Laban's would be white and Jacob's would be blemished. "Let me go through all your flocks today and remove from them every speckled or spotted sheep, every dark-colored lamb and every spotted or speckled goat." (Genesis 3-:32).

There is not just an element of genetics applied to animal breeding in this story, there is also an element of indigenous medicine. Once Jacob's herds were separated, he started feeding poplar, almond and plane tree bark to his ewes, blended into their drinking water. These trees are known to increase reproductive rates. They optimize gestation, thus increasing conception rates. They also have other medicinal applications to males, making them healthier mates. Jacob cut strips in the twigs, which exposed the tannins in the bark, then he put them in the water troughs, where solar heat probably warmed them up enough to release the chemical compounds into the drinking water.

So what we have here is a combination of social distancing, indigenous medicine and good planning. The result was that Jacob's herds grew phenomenally faster. He had become a successful farm manager. Soon this created the psychological conditions for his departure from Syria, back to the land of Israel, taking both his uncle's daughters with him.

Social distancing has a scientific purpose. Applied to the Covid-19 pandemic in 2020, it is simple to explain. On average one person or "vector" contaminates another 2.5 people. Each of who does the same, exponentially. Over a period of 30 days, that comes to 300 people. If you can cut down the number of people contaminated by each person by 50 percent – to just 1.25 people, the number of people contaminated after 30 days comes to 15. That is a 95 percent reduction.

Soon the virus is only jumping to those who have previously been contaminated, and its spread is diminished. Eventually it will run out. This is the logic of staying at three days' journey apart – in self-isolation (voluntary) or even quarantine (imposed).

Then you have the importance of hygiene or herd health - hand-washing and keeping surfaces where the virus can survive over long periods of time disinfected.

Finally, if infected, you have the need for medical care. Jacob used tree-bark. The Chinese doctors who had no known treatment for Covid-19 reported that they found Hydroxychloroquine to be helpful as a therapeutic. It was not a cure, but it bought some time for the immune system to win the internal battle against the virus. French and Spanish doctors facing the same challenge reported that antibiotics like Azithromycin had the same effect. German and American doctors tried using Remdesivir, an anti-viral drug that had been developed for Ebola. None of these had been vetted by clinical trials, so the "anecdotal evidence" was often dismissed as unscientific. The same was true of intravenous Vitamin C – just a shot in the dark. During the "hammer" phase of the pandemic, doctors were without any known therapeutic or cure. Not to mention a vaccine, which labs were working on frantically, but needed time to develop.

So we all need to do what Jacob did – distance ourselves from our workplace. We can only use the therapeutics that are known to work, even if there has not been enough time to verify that through scientific clinic trials. The indigenous knowledge from South America – that quinine cures malaria – did not come out of laboratories. It was derived from the bark of the Cinchona tree.

There is not one silver bullet. Not yet. So we need to combine strategies as Jacob did – in our case, containment, contact-tracing, social distancing and medical care. Keep your distance!

May your future be as bright as Jacob's turned out to be.

The Amorites

Just as there were pockets of monotheists here and there, the patriarchs kept running into the Amorites in their travels too – here and there on both sides of the river Jordan. Once when Abraham travelled down to Egypt, the Pharaoh had intimidated his way into a relationship with Sarah. He became afflicted and thus perceived the error of his ways, when he found out the hard way that Sarah was Abraham's wife. A generation later, Abimelech of Gerar was also angry at Isaac for the same reason. But he was spared for the time being because "the iniquity of the Amorite was not yet full". The fullness of time only came centuries later when the children of Israel return with Joshua to take back their Promised Land.

As Joshua led the children of Israel out of the desert towards Canaan, they encountered two Amorite kings on the east bank of the Jordan. First they defeated a king called Sihon. Then they took out a king called Balak in Moab. Then came that amazing crossing of the Jordan river.

A veteran missionary John Potter creatively presents the five Amorite kings that Joshua had to contend with, in the south of the Promised Land, before going further north to take Jericho. According to his article <u>Adventures with the Amorites</u>, these were:

1. Adoni-Zedek who now ruled Salem (Jerusalem, where Abraham had found Melchizedek). From the righteous descendant of Noah who had welcomed Abraham... to a self-righteous ruler. Only the corrupt play by their own rules. This king's name is equivalent to Mr Self-Righteous.

1. Then came Hohan, king of Hebron. The place where Abraham was buried. His name means "company". This king's name is equivalent to Mr Alliance.

1. Next to Piran, king of Jarmuth. His name means "height". For military reasons, kings were safer in citadels. This king's name is equivalent to Mr Incorrigible.

1. On to Japhia, king of Lachish. His name means "high places". He and Mr Incorrigible were the original "hill billies"! This king's name is equivalent to Mr Pride.

1. Last of all was king Debir at Eglon. His name is about "speaking". Maybe he had the gift of the gab? Or maybe he was already possessed of the spirit of Bel or Baal? He is the dark lord of the "persuasive voices". This was a really long and extended battle, where famously the sun stood still to help Joshua's forces to prevail. This king's name is equivalent to Mr Wraith.

I have met new incarnations of these same five characters – fronting for the same rulers of the darkness. It is always hardest to defeat Mr

Wraith. It takes a lot of time, but victory always belongs to the Lord. They can collude and collaborate against you, too, like Mr Alliance. And they deny any wrong-doing like Mr Pride. Without naming names, I think that it would be reasonably easy to find a Mr Self-Righteous, a Mr Alliance, a Mr Incorrigible, a Mr Pride and a Mr Wraith in the Cabal that brought us State Capture. I will leave it to your imagination to come up with some nominations. State Capture is an enemy and it needs to be defeated, decisively. Again. Because in the on-going cosmic struggle, they are but fronting for the "principalities and powers" and the "rulers of the darkness of this world". They keep on keeping on, and they continue to enlist leaders to be their fronting, who will build graven images or godless ideologies to force the hoi poloi to worship.

Elijah

No discussion of prophecy would be complete without an honourable mention of Elijah. He is the quintessential voice "speaking truth to power". His name brings to mind images of droughts and storms – so often weather is the way that God intervenes in human history. Sending the flood is but one of many examples in the Bible and in church history of climatic episodes. In a book called <u>God Speaks Through Hurricanes</u>, Daniel Harrison has gathered many examples of this together. For example, he writes: *"Turning to the life of Elijah we find him on a certain occasion prophesying to Ahab, the king of Israel.. '.. there shall not be dew nor rain these years, but according to my word.' (I Kings 17: 1) the king had forsaken God's commandments and followed Balaam instead."*

Elijah's stories ring true with whistle-blowers and activists today... Elijah hiding in a cave; hearing a mighty wind, followed by an earthquake, followed by a fire; ravens bringing him food to eat until the brook dried up; and seeking refuge in a widow's home. I get occasional emails from an NGO in South Africa called Abahlali baseMjondolo (Land and Dignity). They hide, they suffer, their activists are hunted down because they confront government injustices openly – on behalf of the poor. It happens internationally too – think Jamal Khashoggi.

The author Daniel Harrison warns: *"Rather than seeing ourselves as clay in the hands of the Potter, Christians have come to view God as the clay.. as though he may be moulded and made to do.. (what) the people desire.. it is something that has crept into the church unnoticed."*

If we no longer see God as Lord of the weather, have we tamed him into a new image?

David - Rebuking the King

It was the prophet Nathan who rebuked King David, in the golden age of Israel, for his crime against Uriah. The king was caught out by intent – Jamal Khashoggi style. Just so that he could have his way with Bathsheba. This king with many animals in his herds, went and plundered an animal from a poor man's herd to feast on. It was immoral and illegal, and in those days, prophets existed to rebuke kings. (As well as to anoint them, as another prophet Samuel had once done to David.) This was an early version of " checks and balances".

Christians far and wide must accept seeking justice as a biblical norm, and not shun its prophets and columnists for *rebuking the king*. This is part of ministry. A quiet church will find itself drowning in the rising tide of liquid evil. We have to speak up like the Unburdening Panel of the SACC did. *Faith*fully not fearfully.

Solomon

This year's Feast of Tabernacles starts today. Deriving from north of the equator, it was and is a harvest festival. As it happens, Monday is also Thanksgiving Day in Canada. So even though it is springtime in South Africa, we can still pause to give thanks.

It is also a season of making foreigners feel welcome in the land. Tabernacles is unique in that the Gentile nations were invited to come up to Jerusalem along with the Jewish people to worship the Lord at this "appointed time". The Lord told Moses to gather all men, women and children, *along with the foreigners in their land*, so they can learn to fear the Lord (Deut. 31: 12).

When Solomon later dedicated the Temple at Sukkot, he asked the Lord to hear the prayers *of any foreigners* that would come there to pray (II Chronicles 6: 32-33). So this is a season for all of us to work together in South Africa, no matter what boundaries or distinctions may try to separate us.

This is a challenge and possibly a rebuke to the way some South Africans treat foreigners?

Nebuchadnezzar and Belshazzar

One of the pagan gods in the Babylonian pantheon of deities was Nebo, the father of all persuasive voices. He was a Chaldean god whose worship was introduced into Assyria. *"Bel bows down, Nebo stoops low; their idols are borne by beasts of burden. The images that are carried about are burdensome, a burden for the weary."* (Isaiah 46:1).

So Nebo is also an idol. To this idol was dedicated the great temple whose ruins are still seen at Birs Nimrud. A statue of Nebo was found at Calah, which was said to weep tears. It is now in the British Museum.

Nebo is also a place. "Go up into the Abarim Range to Mount Nebo in Moab, across from Jericho, and view Canaan, the land I am giving the Israelites as their own possession." (Deuteronomy 32: 49) "Woe to Nebo, for it will be ruined. Kiriathaim will be disgraced and captured; the stronghold will be disgraced and shattered." (Jeremiah 48: 1) It was a town in Benjamin, probably the modern Beit Nubah, about 7 miles north-west of Hebron. The "children of Nebo" (Nehemiah 7: 33) were of those who returned from Babylon to this location. I am guessing that some of the exiles who returned had syncretized some of the Babylonian culture and religion?

We cannot abide the "persuasive voices" any longer. *Did God say that if you eat this fruit you will die? Didn't God say that if you throw yourself down from the Temple, he will raise you up?*

"Unity" is a political word that comes straight from this demon. *Aren't we all the same? Can't we all rule South Africa together?* Do not listen to the persuasive voices of Nebo. You just cannot put the people who are fronting for him into the shoes of John Dube or Albert Luthuli.

Note that Nebo is mentioned by Isaiah together with another Babylonian god – Bel. He was and is the Confounder, who was mocked with the phrase "Bel himself will be confounded". Some attribute to him the founding of Babylon or say he was the driving force behind building the tower of Babel. Jeremiah did not hold his righteous indignation back:

Announce and proclaim among the nations,
lift up a banner and proclaim it;
keep nothing back, but say,
'Babylon will be captured;
Bel will be put to shame,
Marduk filled with terror.
Her images will be put to shame
and her idols filled with terror.'
(Jeremiah 50: 2)

It goes without saying that king Nebuchadnezzar was named after Nebo and his grandson king Belshazzar was named after Bel.

One of the most famous turnovers ever happened to Belshazzar, a king of Babylon. He held a great feast to celebrate his amazing success. The coup de grace was when he called for the chalices robbed from the Jewish Temple in Jerusalem, to imbibe from. During the feast, a hand was seen in the banquet hall, writing on the wall! The prophet Daniel was called in to interpret this spooky event. Daniel read the words "MENE, MENE, TEKEL, UPHARSIN" and interpreted them for the king:

MENE, *God has numbered the days of your kingdom and brought it to an end*

TEKEL, *you have been weighed ... and found wanting*

UPHARSIN, *your kingdom is divided and given to the Medes and Persians*

That very night the Medes and Persians attacked Babylon and this mighty king, grandson of the great Nebuchadnezzar, was out in the bundu hiding behind rocks to escape the enemy. His dynasty was of little use to him anymore, and his favourite gods could not help him.

Without suggesting that Covid-19 is a judgment sent by God (the jury is still out on its biological origins), what it has shown is how fast unforeseen circumstances can change the direction of history. And how much this can affect our perception of existing leadership. God can and does allow other powers (that you might not have expected) to sort out those who try to rebel against His authority and to confound human history. He is constantly trying to re-connect with humans.

There was a lot of in-fighting within the Achaemenid Empire. Stretching from Egypt to Afghanistan it covered much of what we now call the Middle East – except for Saudi Arabia. By percentage of world population, this was the largest empire ever. Contesting its dominance internally were the Persians, the Babylonians and the Assyrians. We cannot escape the fact that today's struggles between and among Iran, Iraq, Syria, Egypt and Eritrea have deep and ancient roots. Notably excluding Saudi Arabia.

Cyrus the Great of Persia replaced Belshazzar, creating the conditions for the rediscovery of monotheism. Cyrus was successes by Xerxes, then Art Xerxes and then Darius II. During this Persian period of domination of Mesopotamia, monotheists like the Jews returned to royal favour. This was the period in which the "Babylonian Captivity" ended. The Jews in exile were allowed to return to the Levant and begin the reconstruction of Jerusalem.

Does it seem strange to you that God would use monotheists like the Medes and Persians to defeat the polytheism of Babylon? Perhaps it is no stranger than bringing the Dutch and British to the Cape, who went on to evangelize sub-Saharan Africa starting from Capetown?

When I think that only one Xhosa decided – long after Johannes van der Kemp's short sojourn near Gaika's kraal – to convert to monotheism and monogamy, I see history repeating itself. I also saw the need - centuries later - to defeat the ruling alliance's cabal of corruption and patronage. But I never forget that in the background, there is a cosmic struggle going on as well. Only those who are full of the Holy Spirit are up to this challenge.

In 2013, I met with an advocate who was selected to write up our Summons against corrupt opponents in a case that we only won in the High Court in Pretoria in early 2020! What a sea-change had come over South Africa during these years! That advocate in 2013 was fatalistic. He explained how the Justice system had been undermined and eroded by corrupt practice and political interference. He told us not to expect a "fair" outcome. The courts had become something of a casino, I was told.

Finally through whistle-blowing and a veritable "citizens revolt", the ruling alliance recalled another President and his replacement announced a New Dawn. In term of governance, South Africa needs nothing less than a resurrection.

Demonology - Archdemons, principalities and unclean spirits

I believe that we do not take "spiritual warfare" as seriously as we should. Perhaps some churches do, like ZCC? But we then critique them for being "syncretistic" or "anti-intellectual".

Satan is not mentioned in the Book of Genesis. It is a serpent that tempts Eve. But during the inter-testamental period (between the Old Testament and the New Testament) the influence of Zoroastrianism seems to have crept in. Possibly because the Medes and Persians "liberated" the Jewish captives and repatriated them to Israel? Namely the figure of Angra Mainyu, who developed into a malevolent entity with abhorrent qualities in dualistic opposition to God. In the apocryphal Book of Jubilees, Yahweh grants his adversary (referred to as Mastema) authority over a group of fallen angels, or their offspring, to tempt humans to sin and punish them.

In the synoptic Gospels, the Devil tempts Jesus in the desert (after his baptism by John) and is identified as the cause of illness and temptation. On the third temptation, the Devil takes Jesus to the top of a tall mountain. There, he shows him the kingdoms of the earth and promises to give them all to him if he will bow down and worship him. Each time Jesus rebukes the Devil and, after the third temptation, he is visited by angels. The Devil's promise to give Jesus all the kingdoms of the earth implies that all those kingdoms belong to him. The fact that Jesus does not dispute the Devil's promise indicates that the authors of those gospels believed this to be true. At that time.

But that of course change at the end of Jesus' life, when he harrowed hell and rose from the dead. That was the turning point. The opposite is now true - the Devil is under our feet and we can view apostasy from a great height. But there is still some rearguard action that we have to contend with.

St Paul writes to the church at Ephesus: "For our struggle is not against flesh and blood, but against the rulers, against the authorities, against the powers of this dark world and against the spiritual forces of evil in the heavenly realms." (Ephesians 6: 12)

The Devil is referred to as a "tempter" (Matthew 4:3), "the ruler of the demons" (Matthew 12: 24), "the God of this Age" (II Corinthians 4: 4), "the evil one" (I John 5:18) and "a roaring lion" (I Peter 5: 8).

In the Book of Revelation, Satan appears as a great red dragon, who is finally defeated by Michael the archangel and cast down from Heaven. He is later bound for one thousand years, but is briefly set free before being ultimately defeated and cast into the Lake of Fire.

In the Koran, "Shaitan" (also known as Iblis), is an entity made of fire who was cast out of Heaven because he refused to bow before the newly-created Adam and incites humans to sin by infecting their minds with evil suggestions (*waswās*).

C.S. Lewis offers some good advice in the introduction to his classic The Screwtape Letters (1942): *"There are two equal and opposite errors into which our race can fall about the devils. One is to disbelieve in their existence. The other is to believe, and to feel an excessive and unhealthy interest in them. They themselves are equally pleased by both errors and hail a materialist or a magician with the same delight."* (p. 3)

We probably err on the side of disbelieving. I don't think that even from a high mountain in Israel you could possibly see all the kingdoms of the earth. My reading is that the tempter was the archdemon in that "principality". That is, he was a prince of demons, although not necessarily the one and only adversary. Jesus is seen often enough having authority over lesser demons or evil spirits. But he would not have sensed real temptation if this tempter was not higher ranking than most!

When St Paul writes about "principalities and powers" I believe that archdemons do have territories. In fact, I recall that some mission stations were located only after a kind of mapping had been done. One sangoma (i.e. inyanga) in Mozambique just south of the Zambezi river was particularly potent, judging by his fierce reputation. Thus the Elim Mission was strategically situated on the Zimbabwe/Mozambique border. In those days, protestant missions were not welcome in (catholicized) Mozambique, so missions were often located in rural areas, near the colonial borders. This made cross-border outreach possible in the early days of mission work, when borders were not as well enforced as they are in this day and age. My point is that a principality probably existed long before the Council of Berlin when borders were agreed on. Its force stretched well into Zimbabwe and this caused the site for that Pentecostal mission to be chosen. The proximity was intentional. It was a strategic move in terms of spiritual warfare. And it provoked a fierce response in due course – for the Elim missionaries later had to relocated to the Vumba mountain for security reasons. Where they were all martyred, not long afterwards.

I suspect that there is a prince of darkness whose rule stretches along the east coast of Africa. His influence reaches as far north as the border of Ethiopia (which has been largely monotheist for 3000 years). It runs down the east coast all the way to the Eastern Cape. The first Christian to evangelize the southern tip of this principality was the fearless Johannes van der Kemp, during the short period that he stayed among the Xhosa, near Gaika's kraal. While there, he prayed that the gospel would spread north, deep into Africa. His prayers have been answered.

The predominantly Bantu people of this area may use other names for these rulers of darkness, but I wonder if they are not Nebu and Bel? Who once ruled through Nebuchadnezzar and his grandson Belshazzar. I believe that *stoicheon* like these rule through proxies like those two Babylonian kings. Probably the Amorite kings before them were their proxies too? And very possibly the Cabal of corrupt leaders in South Africa have been more proxies?

I see horizontal stages as well as a vertical. Vertically, it is a figure like Angra Mainyu at the top – the Devil. Under him are the archdeacons. Under them are demons. And under them are unclean spirits. At the same time, horizontally, these "rulers of the darkness of this world" like to be worshipped through idols. Like the ancient statue of Nebo that was said to shed tears. These days, ideologies may be worshipped more than idols? But if they are godless, they may not just be "secular" as they claim to be. That could be part of the deception?

But the real "fronting" for these dark powers comes from human rulers – like Nimrod, then the Amorite kings, then the Babylonian kings, then some Bantu chiefs and/or sangomas, and now through corrupt leaders in cabal within a constitutional democracy. They actually tried to capture the State! When these proxies are dashed like Belshazzar, as foretold by Daniel when he interpreted the writing on the wall, they may relocate. Most conveniently to another polytheist setting - because under monotheism they tend to get sidelined. Disbelieving this perception of reality only gives away the advantage. Maybe they moved south into Africa?

Archdemons

Archdemons are described as the leaders of demonic hosts, just as archangels lead choirs of angels. The writings of St Paul give some clues. For example in his letter to the church at Colossae: "For in him all things were created: things in heaven and on earth, visible and invisible, whether thrones or powers or rulers or authorities; all things have been created through him and for him." (Colossians 1: 16) And to the church at Ephesus: "he raised Christ from the dead and seated him at his right hand in the heavenly realms, far above all rule and authority, power and dominion, and every name that is invoked, not only in the present age but also in the one to come." (Ephesians 1: 21)

Based upon the writings of Saint Paul the angelic court was described by Pseudo-Dionysius the Areopagite as comprising of nine orders of angels. Three hierarchies with three orders each. The first hierarchy consists of: Seraphim, Cherubim and Thrones. The second hierarchy consists of: Dominions, Virtues and Powers. The third hierarchy consists of: Principalities, Archangels and Angels. This system of classifying angels has been accepted by the majority of Christian scholars. However, no similar consensus has been reached on the classification of demons. This is largely due to the fact that, historically, the definition of what an archdemon is and the names of those demons has varied greatly over time. Also, why would one army organize its opponent? We can only gather glimpses of intel.

One common medieval classification associated the seven deadly sins with archdemons:

- Pride - Lucifer
- Greed - Mammon

- Lust - Asmodeus
- Envy - Leviathan
- Gluttony - Beelzebub
- Wrath - Satan
- Sloth - Belphegor

The pagan deity Ba'al was reinterpreted as the archdemon Bael or Beelzebub. It is misleading to speak of just the Adversary, or the Devil, or the Anti-Christ, as if they are only one. Second, the name Bel never seems to be far from the pantheon or hierarchy. New archdemons were invented over time, from six in Zoroastrian doctrine, to seven in the medieval church's list. They are always associated with degrading the behavior of humans. In Book V of Against Heresies, Iranaeus addresses the figure of the Anti-Christ referring to him as the "recapitulation of apostasy and rebellion." Nebo and Bel come to mind.

Where did Nebo and Bel go to after Beshazzar's Feast?

Nebo and Bel may have relocated, under the ascent of monotheism in Mesopotamia? Remembering that term "principalities", you do have princes of darkness ("rulers of the darkness of this world"). This implies territories, and I suspect that Nebo and Bel moved south.

Veteran missionaries in South Africa have told me that there is a demonic force who has authority all the way to Kenya. I always wondered about that, or how they would know that? But I think I have come to a very rational explanation. I will try to just outline it in 18 steps.

1. In the pantheon of Babylonian gods, Nebo was/is the god of the persuasive voices. Nebuchadnezzar was his namesake.
2. Bel was/is the Cofounder. Belshazzar was his namesake.
3. Belshazzar's mother was the daughter of Nebuchadnezzar. So Nebuchadnezzar was his grandfather.

4. Belshazzar's famous feast brought Daniel into the narrative. He was an expat, who worshipped a "foreign" God (as if the Creator can be "foreign" at any place in Creation).

5. The same night that he/they saw the writing on the wall, they were put to the sword by the Medes and Persians under Cyrus the Great.

6. The Persians were die-hard monotheists, namely Zoroastrians. Zarathustra got rid of polytheism in what is today Iran. So the defeat of Belshazzar that night was also the defeat of polytheists by monotheists. It was the end of Belshazzar but in the heavenlies, Bel lost a lot of prestige and moved on.

7. After the Babylonian captivity, only 11 of the 12 tribes of Israel returned "home" (west). The twelfth tribe travelled south to what we now call Yemen. Much later they migrated south (possibly under pressure from the rise if Islam?) along the coast and went up the Zambezi River to a place called Sena. From there they migrated slowly south and stopped at Burgersfort, in what is now Limpopo province. There is a tribe there that has always practiced and preached circumcision and other Old Testament habits. They have strongly influenced African-Initiated Churches like ZCC. Blood research has verified that these people are Semites not Bantus.

8. Saudi Arabia remained polytheist until the time of Mohamed. He was the one who (sometimes by force) converted the Saudi peninsula to Islam. This is probably around the time (maybe the cause) that the twelfth tribe headed south along the African coast? Mohammed also tried to convert Ethiopia, but it clung to orthodox Christianity.

9. In Ethiopia, on the other side of the Red Sea, monotheism had taken root early. It was polytheist until the Queen of Sheba returned from visiting Solomon. Then she converted her whole nation to Judaism. It was practiced there for 1000

years before it started converting to Christianity, after Philip baptized the Ethiopian ruler in the Book of Acts.

10. So the scenario is this - from Zoroastrian Persia across to the Levant to Egypt and Ethiopia, it was a checkboard of monotheism and polytheism. When the Medes and Persian conquered Babylon, Bel and his namesake Belshazzar recognized that monotheism was on the ascendency.

11. Nebo and Bel were among the "rulers of the darkness of this world". They had to find another context to emerge in, with their "persuasive voices" and confounding. They were looking for a polytheist environment, so they moved down the African coast. Right past monotheist Ethiopia to Kenya, and on down! This new zone of influence included Nilotics (Somalis, Dinka, Nuer, waTutsi) and of course Bantus. These are two different black races.

12. Gradually, Bantus had crossed from origins around Nigeria - to Kenya. Thence they migrated / expanded south. They eventually reached down as far as the Eastern Cape.

13. Johannes van der Kemp, a pioneer missionary here in South Africa, reached Capetown in 1799. There were no Bantus there then. There were Khoisan (then called Hottentots) and Malay and Malagassy slaves, brought back from the east by the Dutch traders. Van der Kemp had to travel very far to the east – overland - to visit and evangelize "blacks" (called by "the k word" at that time). He was well received by King Gaika of the Xhosa, compared to the reception that he had received from the Boers. My only point here is that monotheism was starting to trek north from the Cape - in differing versions whether Boer or missionary.

14. After van der Kemp's death about 10 or 15 years later, one of Gaika's advisors named Ntsikane did decide to convert to Christianity. He thus stepped out of polygamy and into

monogamy as well. He became one of the church fathers of South Africa, but to do so he had to move away from Gaika's kraal. Those persuasive voices were too strong in the heart and mind of Gaika, who resisted conversion.

15. The gospel spread north through the Xhosas, the Zulus, the Swazis and the Sothos. It came inland too - through Xangan country (now southern Mozambique).

16. Now the favourite context of Nebo and Bel – polytheism - was caught between the Ethiopian Orthodox church to the north of Kenya, and this tide of monotheism coming north from Xhosa country, and inland from the Indian Ocean side.

17. God called pioneer missionaries right into the midst of this context - north of Swaziland which had largely Christianized. They travelled all the way up to Malawi and even visited Kenya. They keenly sensed the spiritual warfare that we are still waging in our work here. For the mix of monotheism and constitutional democracy do not align well with Nebo's persuasive voices and Bel's confounding.

18. My view in this part of the world is that Nebo and Bel are about to be ejected again, as they once were by the Medes and Persians from Babylon, when they defeated Belshazzar. They have to go somewhere else, to move on – but where to? Maybe they should go to another planet?

2. A VOICE CRYING IN THE VELD

THE Achaemenid Empire was swept away by the Greek conqueror Alexander the Great. This was followed by the rise of Rome, which established provinces in Egypt and Syria. Only later was the remainder of the Levant brought under Roman rule. This was preceded by a major census of that region, which caused Joseph and Mary to travel from Nazareth to Bethlehem to be registered in his home area.

Three decades later, Jesus remarked that the greatest prophet of them all was John the Baptist, who in his estimation preached with the power of Elijah. Soon after, Herod Antipas, the ruler of Galilee, beheaded the imprisoned John the Baptist – because of the rebukes that John had spoken about him. For example, for marrying his brother Philip's wife, Herodias, who basically manipulated Herod into giving the order for John the Baptist's execution.

When news of his demise came to Jesus, "*he left in a boat to a remote area to pray*".

Jesus was a great admirer of a prophet who would "speak truth to power". Of course John was also an aesthetic, one of the "desert fathers" who role-modeled a life-style that St Francis of Assisi would champion over 1000 years later. His preaching was "pro-poor" as we would call it today. When John the Baptist sent messengers from prison to ask Jesus if he was the one whose trail he had blazed, Jesus replied:

"*Go back to John and tell him what you have heard and seen— the blind see, the lame walk, those with leprosy are cured, the deaf hear, the dead are raised to life, and the Good News is being preached to the poor.*" *And he added, "God blesses those who do not fall away because of me.*"

That last phrase that Jesus added was ominous. So many religious leaders preach and teach well ("what you have heard"). And authentic ministry really resonates with the crowds ("what you have seen"). But addressing economic inequality with "development" is an even higher good. And highest of all, in my estimation, are the roles of lobbying and advocacy.

However, austerity is asking a little much, and mendicancy is over the top. And losing our heads to speak truth to power?

John the Baptist was an ascetic	Jesus was a lush
John was based in the wilderness	Jesus had an urban base – from Nazareth to Capernaum to Jerusalem
John was reclusive and exclusive	Jesus engaged, almost as a populist
John called people to repent	Jesus taught people to love their enemies
John practiced baptism	Jesus practiced inclusion and tolerance
John disturbed public leaders	Jesus disturbed religious leaders
John was expecting an apocalyptic messiah and wondered if it was Jesus	Jesus heralded the "reign of God" which could mean morality and ethics

"What should we do then?" the crowd asked. John answered, "Anyone who has two shirts should share with the one who has none, and anyone who has food should do the same." Even tax collectors came to be baptized. "Teacher," they asked, "what should we do?" "Don't collect any more than you are required to," he told them.

Then some soldiers asked him, "And what should we do?" He replied, "Don't extort money and don't accuse people falsely—be content with your pay."

Share your resources with the poor, don't overtax them or extort them. The well-to-do should be content – enough is enough.

The Patron Saint of Fundraising

In <u>A Christmas Carol</u>, Charles Dickens articulates his social comment on Christmas: "At this festive season of the year, Mr Scrooge," said the gentleman, taking up a pen, "it is more than usually desirable that we should make some slight provision for the poor and destitute, who suffer greatly at the present time... We choose this time, because it is a time, of all others, when Want is keenly felt, and Abundance rejoices."

That was 150 years ago! It was after the Industrial Revolution, but before the dawn of Consumerism. In a way, Christmas has been hijacked. It seems to be more of a celebration of Abundance than of the birthday of one who taught:

Congratulations, you poor!
God's domain belongs to you.
Congratulations, you hungry! You will have a feast.
Congratulations, you who weep now! You will laugh.

These *beatitudes* feature the dramatic presentation and reversal of expectations that are characteristic of Jesus. He and Charles Dickens were on one and the same frequency when it comes to the need for social justice and a preoccupation with the poor.

Mind the Gap

A study by the World Institute for Development Economics Research at United Nations University reports that the richest 1% of adults alone owned 40% of global assets in the year 2000. The three richest people possess more financial assets than the lowest 48 nations combined. The combined wealth of the "10 million dollar millionaires" grew to nearly $41 trillion in 2008. Meanwhile, in 2001, 46.4% of people in sub-Saharan Africa were living in extreme poverty. Nearly half of all Indian children are undernourished, however, even among the wealthiest fifth one third of children are malnourished.

The Occupy Movement

The phrase "The 99%" is a political slogan used by protesters of the Occupy Movement. It was originally launched as a Tumblr blog page in late August of 2011. It refers to the concentration of wealth among the top 1% of income earners compared to the other 99 percent; the top 1 percent of income earners nearly tripled after-tax income over the last thirty years according to a Congressional Budget Office report.

The report was released just as concerns of the Occupy Wall Street movement were beginning to enter the national political debate. According to the Congressional Budget Office, between 1979 and 2007 the incomes of the top 1% of Americans grew by an average of 275%. During the same time period, the 60% of Americans in the middle of the income scale saw their income rise by 40%. Since 1979 the average pre-tax income for the bottom 90% of households has decreased by $900, while that of the top 1% increased by over $700,000, as federal taxation became less progressive. From 1992-2007 the top 400 income earners in the USA saw their income increase 392% and their average tax rate reduced by 37%. In 2009, the average income of the top 1% was $960,000 with a minimum income of $343,927. In 2007 the richest 1% of the American population owned 34.6% of the country's total wealth, and the next 19% owned 50.5%. Thus, the top 20% of Americans owned 85% of the country's wealth and the bottom 80% of the population owned 15%.

Culture Jamming

This phenomenon is a form of protest. The term "jam" contains more than one meaning, including improvising, by re-situating an image or idea already in existence, and interrupting, by attempting to stop the workings of a machine. This was the vocation of the prophets, and John the Baptist was the greatest of them all.

We need to recover his message, which Jesus held in high esteem. In fact, not only was John a forerunner of Jesus but his Gospel of Repentance precedes the radical message of inclusion and tolerance that follows it – to the point of loving your enemies. It is predicated on John's missive about sharing and contentment.

Gifts of the Magi

The practice of exchanging of gifts at Christmas is a kind of Mutual Fund. Everybody benefits! In some shops, 50% of annual turnover happens during the season of Christmas shopping. This is not to be confused with agape love or compassion.

Remember that this is a time, of all others, when Want is keenly felt, and Abundance rejoices.

The Magi brought gifts to a baby lying in a manger. The New Testament never says that this was in a stable. It simply says that there was no guest room available. Mangers built from wood are not that different in size or shape from cradles. They are crude, but readily available in an agrarian setting. In today's urban setting it might have happened that Mary laid Jesus in a cardboard box! The point is that they were not well-to-do.

So when the Magi came, it was a case of grown-ups who were wealthy and wise sharing with a poor and vulnerable child.

The Grinch who restores Christmas

This is a call in the year of the Arab Spring, "culture jamming" and the Occupy Movement, to revise your gift-giving habits.

Beware the hype of advertising! Be content with what you have.

Follow the same star that the Magi did – to a humble setting where "Want is keenly felt".

Don't celebrate Abundance. Affluence is not something to rejoice in, when the disparities outlined above are on the rise.

The Cause of the Month

The annual round of climate talks began this week in Durban, South Africa. The big questions are said to be:

- the fate of the Kyoto Protocol
- emissions reduction targets
- how to bridge the divide between rich and poor

Don't ask "What can Durban deliver?"

Ask what *you* can deliver, this month – to those where Want is keenly felt. That is where the road out of Global Warming begins.

3. THE SERVANT KING

Keep the Herod in Christmas

The story of the "massacre of the innocents" is left out of the Gospels that were written later. Presumably because it is so brutal? But there are distinctions between Herod and the "new-born king" that are important to make...

The first and obvious one is their age. Herod is old and his reputation is in tatters. Only three decades later, when he reached the age of 30, the "new-born king" emerged as a prominent religious leader *speaking truth to power*. He was silenced when he was 33 years old.

Samora Machel was 42 years old when he became President. Patrice Lumumba was 35. Thomas Sankara was 33. They were green. They made mistakes. But their respective countries loved them in spite of themselves, and still do. South Africa needs to move on from its battle-hardened stalwarts to leaders that "think young". Remembering that two-thirds of South Africans are under 35 years of age. So is about half of the Electorate.

Second and equally obvious is the contrast in leadership styles – the top down despot versus the "servant leader". Herod's palace with its sparsely-populated "corridors of power" versus a manger-bed in a stable as there was no room in the crowded Inn. Jesus would go on to espouse Service not Power as the litmus test of leadership.

We do not just celebrate the birth of a new leader. We celebrate the birth of *a new way of leading*.

In their book The Fall of the ANC, Mashele and Qobo call the breed of leaders that became typical after Polokwane as "vindictive triumphalists". It is not a pretty phrase. But it pretty much suits Herod!

Then there are the "soul-battered mourners", according to Mashele and Qobo. Indeed. Those who keep to themselves – like shepherds. Those who immerse themselves in the future not in the present – like the Magi. They see extra-terrestrials in light shows in the sky and dream dreams of warning. They are used to slipping out of harm's way, and waiting it out.

Third, it is also a reminder that one criteria to evaluate leaders by, is how children are treated on their watch. Tell that to the bombers of Aleppo. Oliver Tambo said that a nation that does not take care of its youth has no future. And doesn't deserve one.

These are strong words but the Inequality Gap that everyone now agrees is writ large in South Africa is largely a "generation gap". It is true that there is such a thing as "white monopoly capital". It is also true that there is an "age monopoly" as well, with both blacks and whites on both sides of the gap.

More has to be done, by more citizens, for more South African youth and children.

Good is the enemy of great. South Africa can boast some good leaders. They have made some mistakes, but kept the Democracy project going and growing. But South Africa deserves better. It is time for some great leaders to emerge.

In the United States, names like Thomas Jefferson and Alexander Hamilton only waxed into prominence a generation after the Declaration of Independence - when the leading lights like George Washington were waning. There are great leaders among the 55 million citizens in this country today. We need to find them, using the three criteria that emerge from the contrast between Herod and the new-born king. But we may not find them where you would expect.

Pretty much all the issues and challenges facing South Africa boil down to one thing – *leadership.*

Martha and Mary

A familiar motif in scripture contrasts two sisters: Martha, who constantly busied herself with practical, caring, logistical love for her "padre", and Mary, who went to great lengths to be with him, who anointed his feet with expensive oil and dried it with her hair. Mary's extravagance agitated Martha, but both of them really cared for him in their own way. We need to find a balance between the two extremes of pietism and activism - loving God through prayer and worship, and by loving our neighbour. The padre's brother described looking after widows and orphans as "pure religion". Churches in Africa should encourage both modes - *engagement* and *escape*.

Christians have tended to be more comfortable with the idea of God pretending to be man than man pretending to be God. Did you ever wonder why many people who knew Jesus - even half of his own siblings - didn't recognise that he was the Son of Righteousness? I mean, couldn't they tell by his halo, or what?

One heresy which was prevalent in the early church was espoused by Jews who believed that Jesus was just an ordinary man who was temporarily inhabited by the Spirit. These *Ebionites* reckoned that, while he did suffer on the Cross, by that time the Spirit had left his body. They erred on the mortal side - that Jesus was a man pretending to be God. It is still difficult to grasp that while he was fully human, he was fully divine at the same time.

Another heresy - *Docetism* - was opposite to the Ebionites. *"Docetism taught that Christ during his life had only a phantasmal body and not a real one, and that his sufferings were therefore illusory."*

This was the first major swing of the pendulum - to the escape side. There is a tendency to devalue the full humanity of Jesus - a fundamental doctrine - with a notion that he was really God pretending to be man. Perhaps it makes it easier for us to cope with his passion?

It was an eastern Christian, Ignatius, Bishop of Antioch (one of the sub-apostolic fathers), who first dealt with this heresy in one of his seven epistles written en route to Rome, where he was martyred soon after - only eighty years after Jesus ascended. Ironically, in his attempt to put out this fire, he came down very solidly in favour of a strong clergy - a hierarchical trend which in the long run weakened the church. His case for the genuine pain and suffering felt by Jesus is articulate and moving, including mention of the post-resurrection meal: "He ate and drank with them as one in the flesh." Then he shares a penetrating insight. The Docetists, Ignatius observes, *"have no concern for love, none for the widow, the orphan, the afflicted, the prisoner, the hungry, the thirsty... Thus those who deny the gift of God find death in their contending. Let them rather love that they may rise again."*

Is this same critique not similar to the Great Reversal at the end of the nineteenth century? Tremendous momentum in faith-centered advocacy for social and economic justice was swiftly conceded to other ideologies such as scientific socialism and secular humanism; conservative Christians dropped the ball, and retreated into a spiritual shell. For a long time, they/we rode at the back of pluralism's bus. If socialism is now a spent force, can the African church avoid losing that momentum to fulfill its holistic mission in the emerging post- modern era?

As Ignatius rightly observed in the days of the early church, you don't take the humanity of Jesus seriously if you ignore the social, material and economic dimensions of ministry. *You deny the gift*, to use his phrase. "Let them rather love that they may rise again." The pendulum is swinging again as conservative Christians have in recent decades rediscovered the importance of compassionate ministries, economic justice, and peace-making – moving towards the engagement side.

Then along came *Gnosticism*, influencing young Christianity in a big way. In fact, this heresy infected the church for several centuries, affecting its views profoundly. It considered physical matter to be evil, which led to asceticism, and eventually to monasticism. Another pendulum swing - towards the escape side.

Gnostics were echoed by *Montanism*, whose leading proponent became Tertullian of Carthage. It was the first major withdrawal into a shell of emotionalism and holiness, and rejected philosophy and apologetics. Once again the clergy's hand was strengthened, this time by Montanists emphasizing the priest's celebration of the sacraments, and de-emphasizing the preaching of the Word. The process of alienating the laity was speeding up as the pendulum lingered on the escape side.

"Almost invariably in the church's history a heresy has been followed by another exactly opposite, which is at first not seen as a heresy because it is opposite. Thus, at its beginnings, **Arianism** *was tolerated because it was an attack on Sabellianism.*

Sabellianism *had so obscured the distinction between the persons of the Trinity as practically to abandon the doctrine, and Arius claimed to be reasserting it; and he did indeed distinguish the Son from the Father."*

The pendulum was swinging back towards the notion that Jesus was a creature, not the Creator - a man pretending to be God. An African named Athanasius joined the Arians. No less than five times was he banished to a remote region, only to be recalled to Alexandria! This city, which had been graced by other prominent apologists like Clement and Origen, felt the pulses of the pendulum swinging back and forth between opposing views. Athanasius personified engagement.

Then the emperor Constantine intervened. He summoned all the bishops from the East and the West (no one yet thought in terms of the North and the South) to a council in 321 AD, and the Nicene formula was agreed to, even though the controversy continued for some time: "Very God of Very God, begotten, not made". Many delegates at this council bore the scars of persecution, which had only recently abated. Many came from Africa. They were true martyrs, although you would never know it from the way they sometimes behaved. Imagine having the head of state arbitrate a debate among church leaders in a new and unfamiliar alliance! Theology by diplomacy?

Neither did it end the debate, which has rumbled on for centuries. You still meet Christians who have doubts about the divinity of Jesus. Or that there was anything miraculous about his birth.

The Yogi and the Commissar

In the 20th century, the opposite extremes of the pendulum's swing were popularized as the *Yogi* (escape) and the *Commissar* (engagement), images coined by Arthur Koestler. The Yogi derives change from internal sources, much like those who believe that Jesus was God pretending to be man. The Commissar, on the other hand, changes external structures to bring about renewal - more like man pretending to be God.

As eastern mysticism penetrates western society, it oversimplifies matters to suggest that the Commissar (scientific approaches, organizational skills, technology) is paramount.

Likewise, know-how and ideologies from the West have penetrated the East as never before. New formulas and blends are being tested and integrated as they were at Nicea and other Councils where East met West.

Hopefully, orthodoxy will recover a true holistic and redemptive balance by preaching good news to the poor, freedom for the prisoners, recovery of sight for the blind, release to the oppressed, and the acceptable year of our Lord (i.e Jubilee). One side-show in this controversy was the Great Debate which see-sawed between two Christian authors in America. First came Ron Sider's **Rich Christians in an Age of Hunger** in the 1970s. It created a minor sensation in conservative protestant circles. In the 1980s, it was answered by David Chilton's **Productive Christians in an Age of Guilt-Manipulators.** Hmmmm! The pendulum began to swing vigorously, with second and third editions of these books.

Sider was a sort of Commissar, ready to impose "social" solutions for the common good, such as wealth redistribution, and to intervene where necessary to level out the playing field. He was and is for engagement - wanting a New Deal (to speak in American terminology). Ironically, he is a pastor with a soft heart and a wonderful way with words.

Chilton, on the other hand, favored escape - especially from the state playing God in the marketplace. He believed in a "hands-off" approach - that the right approach is self-propelled wealth generation. He was a kind of Yogi - a bible thumper - and he used his bible to thump Ron Sider. Ironically, he was the economist, and he tore into Sider's book with technical skill as well. He mixed economic jargon with a strong dose of scripture.

Sider *the Commissar* seemed to be heavily influenced by populism or even welfare-statism. At least Chilton *the Yogi* didn't retreat into a protective shell of emotionalism (although he got overly zealous at times). His technical competence seemed to be matched by his knowledge of scripture. His rigorous use of Old Testament principles was refreshing. His testiness was not unlike the Arians in the face of formidable odds - the majority which subscribed to the opposite view. By hanging tough like Athanasius did, Chilton really influenced the methods used by Christians "to preach good news to the poor". He did not cause them to escape social responsibility altogether. But to deal with poverty, responses were centred on micro-loans not welfare. To deal with famine, the emphasis was on distributing seeds, not food-aid.

What Sider and Chilton did seem to agree on is that Christians must get involved in alleviating poverty, facilitating development, addressing justice issues, and so on. What they were really disputing was *how to do it*. Similarly, Christians who believe that external aid has weakened Africa, have to grapple with the alternatives. The path to recovery lies neither in top-down nor outside-in approaches, but through internal renewal and self-help.

We need to remember that Jesus - the new Adam - was not all that indistinguishable from ordinary everyday people. If you are scandalised by this notion - ask yourself: are you a closet Docetist? Does your faith stem from the Yogi rather than the Commissar? Do you try to avoid "holy worldliness"? The litmus test is whether your faith translates into action.

What in the world are you doing for Christ's sake?

"Neither the Commissar nor the Yogi, neither the radical Christian reformer nor the Pentecostal are able to solve the problems of our society. The great task of the minister, rather, is to live and to help live in the tension between both and search for a synthesis. The Christian agent of social change is called upon to be a reformer and a man who does not lose his own soul - a man of action and a man of prayer at the same time. He is called upon to be concerned about the large issues of our time without losing sight of the children, the poor, the sick, and the old, who ask for our personal care and attention...

Only the synthesis between the Commissar and the Yogi makes it possible, therefore, to be a real agent of social change... Only this synthesis allows us to look beyond all political, social and economic developments in order to keep us forever awake and always waiting for a new world to come." (Henri Nouwen, Creative Ministry)

Neither is it any longer an east-west synthesis. People of the South must not become so heavenly minded that they are no earthly good. In the North, materialism and secularism are ascendant - something we need to remember as we interact with donors and aid agencies. As we look for balance, let us not exchange our current imbalance (too spiritual) for theirs (too material). We should try to correct the fallacy which regards practical and compassionate ministry as the opening act for the main event of evangelism or "reaching the unreached".

Questions are being raised about both escape and engagement. Holistic balance means more piety when there is too much practicality, and visa versa. While there are advantages to responding corporately, there are dangers in it too. Institutional intervention can go over the top, marginalising genuine, caring Christians who have a lot to give. The debate about whether to redistribute wealth to the poor or enable them to generate it for themselves, sidesteps a critical issue; where does the corporate social responsibility end and personal outreach begin?

At the inter-personal level, rank and file Christians get caught in this crunch. As one activist remarked: "So I have taken to being in the outer circle everywhere it seems. Among fellow business men, I am the guy with the placard beneath his shirt about the rich robbing the poor. Among the poor, I am the guy with the coach's T-shirt underneath, which says my true home is in the suburbs. Among the evangelicals, I am the guy who is leaning left and among the social workers, I am the guy with the Bible in the glove compartment of his car."

The Parable of the River Emergency

The need to balance pietism and activism in the family of faith is one thing. But there is another talking point - a distinction needs to be made between different kinds of Activism. To do this, a parable is related...

Once upon a time there was a village, built on the fertile banks of a river. The villagers could fetch firewood in the forest behind the village, or go hunting there. They could grow food gardens along the alluvial plain, and fish in the river. They were never short of water in this idyllic location.

Then one day, bodies were found to be floating down the river – some dead, some injured. The villagers mobilized their boats and ropes to rescue the perishing. A refugee camp was set up at the shore to welcome them. There was first aid and a soup kitchen. There were tents and blankets. This was called a Relief operation, for it was a humanitarian Emergency.

The Village Council felt that it was a bit condescending to be giving hand-outs to people, so they parceled out some land for them to have gardens and grow their own food. They provided tools for the refugees to go into the forest and cut trees with which to build their own homes in the area downstream from the village. A credit programme was set up to lend them some money to start businesses, to grow the village economy. These were called Development projects.

But more and more bodies kept floating down the river, until the refugee population was growing to outnumber the villagers. So the Town Council deliberated, and decided to send a delegation of villagers on a hike upstream. Their mission was to determine what conflict was causing these injuries and deaths, and to try to intervene and if possible make peace. This came to be called Advocacy or Public Engagement. Some call it "the ministry of justice and peace". In the colloquial sense of the words, these were the *Activists*.

The meaning of the parable is clear. All of the interventions were good. But if you consider going after the causes instead of the symptoms the higher good, then Emergency is an inferior good, and even Development projects are not good enough.

Plans and Premonitions

In what we now call Holy Week, Jesus must have been acutely aware of the risk – if not the inevitability – of his life ending. The gospels even record him predicting it, long before his triumphal entry into the city of Jerusalem on Palm Sunday. The way that he sent some disciples to fetch that donkey that he rode suggests that there were plans if not just premonitions in the background to the narrative. It reminds me of Psalm 39, verses 4 – 6:

Show me, Lord, my life's end
and the number of my days;
let me know how fleeting my life is.
You have made my days a mere handbreadth;
the span of my years is as nothing before you.
Everyone is but a breath,
even those who seem secure.
Surely everyone goes around like a mere phantom;
in vain they rush about, heaping up wealth
without knowing whose it will finally be.

These words rang true to me as I read this psalm this morning. It reminded me that we are living out a "death bed mentality" in the midst of the Covid-19 pandemic, more than ever. That is, living every day as if it was our last. Certainly for someone who is turning 69 this month, and who has underlying health conditions such as Type 2 diabetes, I have to be realistic. Especially as I watch a Prime Minister aged 55 being assisted in intensive care, in a country with far better facilities, and far less inequality.

The gospel writers seem to be aware that there were plans and premonitions in the deep background of Holy Week. They kept mentioning these little glimpses of it. Likewise, I have been quietly and thoughtfully trying to spell out some of my end-of-life desires and preferences – living each day of "lockdown" in the realistic awareness of the risks and hazards of this pandemic. This pathogen is especially dangerous to older people and those who have underlying health concerns.

The personal plans and premonitions I am sharing only with family and close friends. I have no expectation of receiving state-of-the-art medical support. Nor of a Joseph of Arimathea coming forward at the last minute with a free grave. So I have to be realistic, like Jesus was. And make preparations. He knew what was going on right up to the end, and my prayer - like his - is that the Lord might let this cup pass from me, hunkered down in self-confinement.

The prospects are dim for Africa, and South Africa's infection rate is just now starting to climb at Easter time. Government has taken measures promptly and is preparing for the worst. But like Jerusalem in Holy Week, the currents and cross-currents are unpredictable. We do know how it will end, eventually, when we pass through the "hammer" phase and arrive at the "dance" phase. We do not know if and when we will reach the level of "herd immunity". Just as the Romans were cruel overlords, this virus is indiscriminate and tends to go after the elderly and more so the men. So it is best to be prepared. Some scenarios are scary.

One thing that I am working away at, in my solitude, is finalizing several manuscripts to send to my publisher. But he too is working from home. So at least he can still generate eBooks. And upload them to his eShop for marketing! They can be delivered to readers as an email attachment, in either MOBI or EPUB format.

If the time has come for me to leave my legacy, this will be it. I don't mean to be melodramatic or spooky. The prospects are not good. There were a series of false hopes – starting with possible protection of that TB vaccine called BCG which most South African citizens have had. There was "anecdotal evidence" that chloroquine might help as a therapeutic, administered only by doctors with an antibiotic Azithromycin. This did not stand up under scientific scrutiny. Then there was some hope in Remdesivir, an anti-viral that had been developed to treat Ebola. Vitamin-C drip seems like the last hope before intubation on a ventilator. Covid-19 has taken out so many people already that we can only pray for shielding and hope that the Angel of Death will pass-over.

During the lockdown, on-line retailers like Takealot in South Africa and Amazon in the USA are not uploading any new products to their catalogue – unless they are "essential" products. So the actual print-media books cannot be sold or delivered until lockdown ends.

The best-selling book of the 19th century, I learned recently, was written by an American called Henry George. He even out-sold Charles Darwin and Karl Marx! After completing Progress and Poverty, George wrote to his father: "*It will not be recognized at first—maybe not for some time—but it will ultimately be considered a great book, will be published in both hemispheres, and be translated into different languages. This I know, though neither of us may ever see it here.*" That's the spirit of my publishing plan while in self-isolation!

4. THE MAMAS & THE PAPAS

Saint Paul

A contemporary of Jesus, maybe 10-12 years his younger, Saul was from Tarsus (a city in what is now Turkey). Saul may have seen Jesus at a distance or just heard about him, before the Crucifixion. But they did not meet face to face until after the Resurrection, on the road to Damascus, and the encounter shook Saul to his foundations.

He emerged from that episode as "Paul", spending about three years in Damascus and Arabia to get his new bearings. This was a period of "social distancing" to let the infamy of his persecution of Christians fade. Then he was presented to the elders at Jerusalem, where he met Barnabas. Then he returned to his home area of Tarsus - for over a decade.

During this decade, the Christian movement was growing, probably from those who disbursed on the Day of Pentecost, each having heard the Good News miraculously in their own tongue. Some returned to North Africa and before long they began to obey the great commission of Jesus to spread the good news. Some from Cyrene in North Africa (e.g. Simon and Rufus) went to the cosmopolitan trading city of Antioch in Syria to help plant a church. It enjoyed phenomenal church growth, unencumbered by the "double conversion" required by the Jewish Christians in Jerusalem.

We see North Africans crossing the Mediterranean today and causing a lot of upheaval on the other side of the sea, in another context. It happened in the first decades of the early church too! In Jerusalem, the followers of Jesus were still called "Nazarenes" as they were essentially a sect of Judaism. Converts had to embrace both Judaism (i.e. circumcision) and also Jesus and Lord (i.e. faith).

But the thriving church in Antioch – planted with the help of African missionaries – challenged those assumptions. It is enough, they argued, to confess faith in Jesus and to be baptized into his church (making a distinction between those who still adhered to the baptism of John, who were gradually being internalized into Christianity.) The term "Christian" (*little Christ*), which was derogatory at first, emerged in Antioch. This all caused quite a commotion, and Barnabas went down to Antioch from Jerusalem to investigate. He was OK with it. Then he went to Tarsus to find Paul to help him disciple this emerging church. They then reported their findings at the Council of Jerusalem, which is regarded by some as the moment when Christianity and Judaism parted ways – both as world religions. Paul was a devout Jew but also a Roman citizen, fluent in the prevalent Greek culture of that time, as well as Hebrew and Judaism. Remember that Judaism is matrilinear – so Paul's mother was Jewish. So his right to Roman citizenship likely came from his father.

To track Paul's biography is to recognize that there was still a price to pay for "rebuking the king". In three different epistles that he wrote (in the New Testament) he relates his own sufferings. He was arrested more than once, but as a Roman citizen he had a right to a fair trial. In due course, his case was transferred to Rome, because he appealed to Caesar, and several books of the New Testament are actually his *Letters from Prison* there.

His pursuit of justice went on for many years, because the emergence of Christianity was clearly a threat to the status quo (both the Jews and the Romans). This complicated his quest for Roman justice.

This week I have been reflecting on a case that we are prosecuting, finally arriving in the High Court in Pretoria. We took a stand against crime, corruption and nepotism – seven years ago! Pursuing justice not in our own province, but in the capital city. Like St Paul.

For much of this time, a concerted effort has been made by the status quo to tarnish our reputation. Fortunately I have not lost my head, been crucified or imprisoned (although I have been arrested and detained – unlawfully). When I see the way journalists like Jamal

Khashoggi have been treated, I shudder. It is still a cruel world, and speaking truth to power can still be hazardous to your health.

As I read the headlines in South Africa these days, more and more indiscretions are being brought to light. Daily. It is beyond belief. When we blew the whistle seven years ago it was just the tip of the iceberg.

But following in the steps of St Paul, we forged ahead, seeking trial and our moment to out the truth. What Minister Pravin Gordhan calls "Project Re-capture" is going to take a very, very long time to clean up (post-state capture). It is getting messy. Heads will roll – hopefully just proverbially speaking. If they don't, it will undermine what little confidence there is left in leadership and the justice system.

<u>Tertullian</u>

So many of the church fathers (and mothers) came from Africa. Of course Africa was but one shore of the Mediterranean Sea, which connected the dots. So it was part and parcel of the Roman world, and the issues about skin-colour would not arise for many centuries, until the days of the Slave Trade. The Romans were cruel, but they were not racist about it.

In Carthage, in the Roman province of Africa, he was trained as both a lawyer and a priest. He broke the force of false charges – for example that Christians sacrificed infants at the celebration of the Lord's Supper and committed incest. He pointed to the commission of such crimes in the pagan world and then proved by the testimony of Pliny that Christians pledged themselves not to commit murder, adultery, or other crimes. He was the first recorded writer to refer to the Trinity.

He challenged the inhumanity of pagan customs such as feeding the flesh of gladiators to beasts. He argued that because there are no "gods" thus there is no pagan religion against which Christians may offend. Christians do not engage in the foolish worship of the emperors, they do better - they pray for them. Christians can afford to be put to torture and to death, and the more they are cast down the more they grow...

"The blood of the martyrs is seed" (Apologeticum, 50)

Perpetua and Felicitas

Rarely have women been venerated by so many, for so long! A 22-year noble woman and a pregnant slave girl were martyred together under the persecution of Septimus. In Carthage a magnificent basilica was afterwards erected over the tomb of these two women martyrs, the Basilica Maiorum, where an ancient inscription bearing their names has been found.

Saints Felicitas and Perpetua are two of seven women commemorated by name in the second part of the Canon of the Mass.

The once-flowering rambling rose "Félicité et Perpétue" (R. sempervirens x 'Old Blush') with palest pinks buds opening nearly white, was introduced by Robert Jacques in 1828.

Two historical fiction novels have been written from the point of view of Perpetua. Amy Peterson's Perpetua: A Bride, A Martyr, A Passion (ISBN 978-0972927642) was published in 2004, and Malcolm Lyon's The Bronze Ladder (ISBN 978-1905237517) in 2006.

"See that pot lying there?" she asked her father. "Can you call it by any other name than what it is?" "Of course not," he answered. Perpetua responded, "Neither can I call myself by any other name than what I am - a Christian."

Cyprian

A new persecution of the Christians began in under Emperor Valerian I, and both Pope Stephen I and his successor, Sixtus II suffered martyrdom at Rome.

In Africa Cyprian courageously prepared his people for the expected edict of persecution by writing a pastoral letter, and set an example himself when he was brought before the Roman proconsul of Carthage, Aspasius Paternus. He refused to sacrifice to the pagan deities.

The consul banished him to Curubis, modern Korba. From there he comforted to the best of his ability his flock and his banished clergy. In a vision he saw his approaching fate. When a year had passed he was recalled and kept under house arrest, in expectation of severer measures after a new and more stringent imperial edict arrived, demanding the execution of all Christian clerics.

He was imprisoned at the behest of the new proconsul Galerius Maximus. The day following he was examined for the last time and sentenced to die by the sword. His only answer was *"Thanks be to God!"*

"He can no longer have God for his Father who has not the Church for his mother"

(De unitate ecclesiae)

5. MEDIEVAL

FROM Nathaniel Bartholomew (i.e. Bar Ptolemy) to Simon of Cyrene – the man who carried the cross of Jesus for him when he could no longer manage by himself – the history of the Christian movement is sprinkled with African heroes of faith. Never can it be said that Christianity was only "a white man's religion". In fact, until after St Paul's "Macedonian call", it was quite otherwise...

St Athanasius

At the age of 27, he assisted Bishop Alexander at the Council of Nicaea, where his influence began to be felt. Five months later, on his death bed, the bishop recommended Athanasius as his successor. He was elected unanimously 5 months later, and at age 30 he became archbishop of Alexandria. He was the chief defender of Trinitarianism against Arianism.

His refusal to tolerate the Arian heresy led to many trials and persecutions. He spent seventeen of the forty-six years of his episcopate in exile. During his lifetime he was engaged in theological and political struggles against the Emperors Constantine the Great and Constantius II and powerful and influential Arian churchmen, led by Eusebius of Nicomedia. Thus he came to be known as *"Athanasius Contra Mundum"*.

"Jesus that I know as my Redeemer cannot be less than God"

St Augustine

He came from cosmopolitan Hippo, in North Africa. As a foodbasket for the capital city of the Empire, it had a thriving Roman presence. There was also a long established Hebrew community there, from which some Biblical figures had emerged – like Barnabas, his sister Mary and her son Mark. Then there was "the Third Way" – the Christian community - which Augustine refused to join for decades, in spite of his mother's prodding and prayers.

Augustine's influence is almost without comparison in church history. At its root is a personal conversion. An about face. A change of heart and mind. Another great African theologian, David Bosch, wrote: "Christianity that doesn't begin with the individual, doesn't begin. But Christianity that ends with the individual, ends." The basis of social renewal is personal renewal. As a changed person, Augustine set about to change the church and society.

"God loves each of us as if there were only one of us."

Mendicancy

I have been reflecting on the mendicant orders. Just like no one wants to eat pig, but they will eat pork - mendicant is a much more refined word for begging.

It started in Africa. An Egyptian, St Anthony was the first of the "desert fathers". Around 300 AD he became a recluse, acting alone, not asking anyone to join him.

The first one to actually organize a monastery was Pachomius, about 320 AD, also in Egypt.

The first monastery in Europe was started by an African – St Athanasius – in about 335 AD. He was in exile, in what is now Germany.

St Martin started the first monastery in France around 350 AD.

St Augustine was the first to form a celibate community, in 395 AD. It was another first for Africa – in Hippo.

St Patrick Christianized Ireland starting in 432 AD, after ministry preparations in Gaul. His use of Abbeys was unprecedented – the Abbots were the main church leaders, as opposed to the European configuration which organized dioceses around bishops.

It was not until around 550 AD that Canadorius deployed monks for the first time in the translation of manuscripts.

During the so-called Dark Ages, around 575 AD, the Celtic Church re-evangelized Europe, founding 40 monasteries. Pope Gregory I noted that the Celtic monks were the first to dress differently, with robes and distinctive haircuts. He was the same pope who promoted the rigorous Benedictine Rules, which had been formulated by an Abbot by that name.

From Self-denial to Self-reliance

A funny thing happened on the way to the forum...

Ignatius, who was the first person to coin the phrase "catholic church", was also the first to distinguish between the offices of bishop, elder (presbyter) and deacon. He saw the bishop reflecting God's role, the elders reflecting the role of church councils, and deacons reflecting the ministry of Jesus. Structure was starting to set in, although a quick look at I Timothy 3 and Acts 15 will confirm that this thinking was in line with practice and teaching in the early church. Like Tertullian, who coined the phrase "trinity", such new concepts and structures were evolving during the turbulent era after the Apostles and before the conversion of the Emperor Constantine, in 312 AD.

In 361 AD, the last pagan emperor ascended. From 363 onwards, all emperors were Christian. At this time there were various bishops and none was paramount. Thus the rise and fall of various heresies and tendencies, as these were debated and defended.

By 390, St Ambrose, bishop of Milan, actually excommunicated the emperor! This was a far cry from a persecuted, underground early church.

Leo I became the first pope – in 440 – by declaring the supremacy of the bishop of Rome. By that time, Patrick was already evangelizing Ireland! There was no pope yet at the time that he set out from Europe to evangelize the emerald isle, where he had previously been captive in slavery.

Bible Translation

Concurrent to these dates was another phenomenon – the emergence of Bibles in the vernacular. This is often associated with the much-later Protestant Reformation about the time that the printing press emerged, but the truth is that several translations had been undertaken long before that.

Armenia was the first nation to declare itself Christian, in 303 AD. By 400 AD, the Bible had been translated into that language.

Around 340 AD, Bishop Ulfilas translated the Bible for the Goths. This is at the root of Gothic influence over church and community life for many centuries – particularly in architecture.

When St Jerome translated Scripture into Latin, in 405 AD, it was still a "live" language. Too often his Vulgate is remembered as part of the "hocus pocus" syndrome that emerged - long after Latin ceased to be spoken in streets and homes, like Hebrew before it. But at the time this translating was done, it was part of a trend have scripture into the vernacular.

So it was only a question of time before Canadorius thought of deploying monks in the translation of manuscripts.

The Peregrini

I have mentioned several times that there were a number of surges or waves of missionary activity after the initial one, when the Twelve Apostles fanned out in all directions from the Levant.

One of these waves came out of Ireland. In this case, the missionaries were already wealthy and powerful, and they led delegations or teams. They travelled across the sea to Scotland, to France, and to Holland. They penetrated into Europe as far as St Gall in Switzerland.

These were men, and they called themselves "the Peregrini". This is because they left Ireland behind, with no intention of ever returning. It was a kind of self-exile, to authenticate their sincerity among those that they came to serve. Those who were not celibate would have to inter-marry with local women.

Similarly, during the Age of Discovery as missionaries were deployed overseas by the London Missionary Society, many left never to return. Those who were rejected in Tonga, for example, went to Australia (called "New South Wales" at the time).

This is not true of all missionaries today. Many see themselves as a kind of diplomatic or military posting – to perform a remit, after which they will return "home" to the North. Often people who think like this try to maintain a living standard – even while on "the field" – that is commensurate with the average in their homeland. This can exacerbate the inequality between them and those they serve. So the degree to which missionaries "go native" varies, and is a bit controversial in mission circles.

Another factor is that there are not only significant differences between the two cultures of home base and mission field, but in either of those settings you will also find significant differences between church culture and the prevailing culture on the street. The church is "in the world, but not of the world". It is commissioned to be a counter-culture in some ways confronting society, as we have noted in its "public engagement" ministry. You might find less of a "gap" between the way church members behave in the two settings – North and South? But almost invariably, there will be some level of inequality.

You will also find Christians in the North critiquing their own society and culture. For example, when Fridtjof Nansen of Norway won the Nobel Peace prize in 1922 for his relief work in Russia during the influenza epidemic, he said of Western civilization that: "the ceaseless turmoils of the cities, and the nightmare of moneymaking is dwarfing the race." So the sending countries do not escape missionary scrutiny!

No Prophet is accepted in his home town

This comment was made by Jesus, but could equally apply to Mohammed, who regarded Jesus as a prophet.

Although Jesus was born in Bethlehem at the time of a Roman census, that was not the family's hometown. Thus we often speak of "Jesus of Nazareth". But the Gospel truth is that Nazareth rejected his prophetic calls – among other things to a radical Year of Jubilee – and he had to slip away before they stoned him.

He moved to Capernaum, where his ministry was based from then on. Capernaum was a port on the Sea of Galilee and thus many of his disciples were fishermen. Whereas Nazareth was up in the hill country, where the family business run by his father was carpentry.

The home of Simon Peter was in Capernaum, where the followers of Jesus often met. Thirty percent of the miracles recorded in the New Testament happened in that house. In later years, a basilica was built over the house on that same site.

Mohammed's hometown was Mecca, a wealthy merchant town. It stood at the crossroads of Asia and the West, Africa and Persia. It connected overland caravan routes with maritime trade via the Red Sea. It also had a famous ancient shrine of pilgrimage called the Kaba, which contained sacred ancient stones including the Black Stone.

It was a cosmopolitan centre where Mohammed came into contact with both Jews and Christians, among others.

Most of the inhabitants of Mecca rejected his prophetic teachings. He encountered rising hostility, and had to relocate to Medina (at that time, it was called Yathrib). This flight is called the "hijrah". This took place in the year 622 of the Christian calendar, although the Islamic calendar starts counting from about this time. Muslim years are dated A.H. ("after hijrah").

Most of its residents were favourably disposed to his message. In the next decade, before the death of Mohammed, Muslim armies conquered the whole of Arabia and stamped Islam on it. This was the first time that the Arabs had ever been unified.

The Islamic calendar (known as the Umm al-Qura calendar) is based on the moon's cycle, whereas the Gregorian one is determined by the sun. For this reason, they are out of sync.

Ramadan is the ninth month of the Islamic calendar. This month commemorates the first revelations to Mohammed by the archangel. Thus it is a month of fasting.

The tenth month is Shawwal. The first day of this month is Eid al-Fitr. Eid means "celebration". It is a feast day. It is actually forbidden to fast on this day.

So Eid Mubarak ("a blessed Eid") to all muSLiM friends... Adore, and draw near to God!

Unravelling

The following centuries see the Roman Church asserting its predominance – over the emperor and the state, the Church of Ireland, the Eastern Church and even crusades against Islam. In the same way, the Vulgate became the paramount translation, even when and where most people no longer understood it! The self-denial of the desert fathers gave way to self-reliance in the monasteries (*ora et labora* – pray and work) and to self-indulgence on the part of bishops and popes. That is the background to the mendicant orders...

From Desert Fathers to Urban Brothers

St Francis of Assisi was quite an amazing person. He saw through it all; self-gratification had replaced self-sacrifice. He questioned the pursuit of wealth and political power – when most people received stones after asking for bread. He looked for a way that was opposite to institutionalization and alliance with the state. This meant that he had to steer clear of both the wealthy Bishops engaged in the intrigues of city life, and also the powerful Abbots whose isolation was no longer in a cave like St Anthony, but in a position that dominated rural life. He started a poverty movement. As Jesus had told his disciples: "If you want to be perfect, go and sell all you have and give the money to the poor, and you will have riches in heaven; then come and follow me." (Matthew 19:21)

"Go and preach, 'The Kingdom of God is near!' Heal the sick, bring the dead back to life, heal those who suffer from dreaded epidemics, and drive out demons. You have received without paying, so give without being paid. Do not carry any gold, silver, or copper money in your pockets; do not carry a beggar's bag for the journey or an extra shirt or shoes or a stick. Workers should be given what they need." (Matthew 10: 7 – 10)

It was a rebuke. There were portents of Ghandi's non-violence in his approach. It was called "mendicant" - that nice word for begging. The Franciscans called themselves brothers, not fathers. They did not retreat into the wilderness, they engaged in community service. They were activists, not just pietists. Their lifestyle was as much a witness as anything. It spoke volumes about their faith. They didn't just believe in miracles, they counted on them.

Post-modern Mendicancy

We live in a different time, but there are parallels. I read in *Wikipedia* this week that Evangelicals now outnumber both Catholics and "main-line" denominations in America. They are only outnumbered by Fundamentalists. But the real discovery for me was that there is now a new movement called the "emerging churches", whose members are referred to as "emergents". While this came as a surprise to me, it is familiar, for the Africa- Initiated Churches (AICs) are a force to be reckoned with in my part of the world. The biggest denomination in South Africa is the Zionist church. It took the gospel from missionaries who came from Zion, Michigan (not Israel!) and like Francis in his era, it re- invented the church. Not only has Africa been Christianized, but Christianity has been Africanized. It sounds like these "emerging churches" are something of a rebuke to the institutional church as well.

But how can you translate scripture, preach (especially in the expensive media), heal, raise the dead, treat dreaded epidemics (especially when anti-retroviral drugs are so expensive) and drive out demons when you have no currency or commodity reserves? You can't even take a guitar case with your guitar – so bunking for money at the subway stations is ruled out! There goes the self-reliance factor of the monasteries.

Jesus has a plain explanation: "Workers should be given what they need." Ya, but by whom? Government? Philanthropic foundations? Churches? Generous people? The beneficiaries?

In today's world, "riches in heaven" is a bit of a pie-in-the-sky-by-and-by. So does fundraising come across as a kind of mendicancy? To beg for resources, you no longer have to take an oath of poverty - the emphasis has shifted to tax deductibility. This certifies two things – that you are a bona fide nonprofit, but also that the donors themselves can benefit from being generous. It gets confusing. I just hope that the emergents can get a handle on it!

Temugen - One person can change the world

1. Who invented paper money to replace coins?
2. Who standardized time and calendar internationally?
3. Who set up the first development agency offering extension services and credit?
4. Who built more bridges than any other conqueror – to move his army across vast distances?
5. Who combined European foundry skills with Persian flame-throwing and Chinese gunpowder to invent a new weapon – the cannon?
6. Who rendered walled cities obsolete?
7. Who first replaced feudal aristocracy with a more egalitarian system based on merit, loyalty and achievement?
8. Who was the first to adopt freedom of worship as a policy of governance?

From deep rural roots, underprivileged, he ended up ruling over ten time zones.

He never went to school, but he ruled the biggest empire of all time - by surface area, by population, and by number of cities and states.

He travelled on horseback, and went on from there to invent postal delivery of mail between far-away cities.

He refused to have his portrait printed, his silhouette imprinted on any coins, and even shunned a memorial grave site. His burial was shrouded in secrecy. Yet we should not forget his inspiring example...

He is Temogen. *The Genghis Khan.*

The Pied Piper of Hamelin

From what little I know about this figure, something of a populist, who came to be associated with the loss of children. Some of those who happily followed him went missing...

He may be associated with the Black Death, which we know now was spread by fleas that normally dwelled on rodents and rats. So getting rid of a rat infestation made the Pied Pieper popular. But then came the social price that Hamelin paid. The meaning of the story is somewhat mysterious, and may have happened already before the Plague arrived?

The academy award for best actor this week went to Forrest Whitaker, for his performance as Idi Amin. At the movie premiere in Kampala, Uganda, president Museveni recalled: "He was always laughing and making jokes, shaking hands and hugging people. He looked like a happy man, someone who should be your friend, but that's how he was able to hide all the terrible things he did."

Amin ruled for eight years, and during that period, 300,000 Ugandans were murdered. That is five people every hour for the whole eight years!

Let me quote an article in today's *Sunday Times* in South Africa, by Duma Gqubule: "Lest we forget, we live in a country where 50 people are murdered and 1000 people die of HIV/AIDS-related diseases every day. By comparison, deaths in the Iraq war last year were 56 people a day. Every two days, more people die in South Africa of HIV/AIDS-related diseases than were killed during the recent war on Lebanon."

"The mismanagement of the epidemic is also mismanagement of the economy, because it has resulted in a massive destruction of human capital. More than two million people have died of HIV/AIDS-related diseases. Most of these deaths could have been avoided. The life expectancy of the average South African has dropped to 50. HIV/AIDS is not a global disease: South Africa, with just 0.7% of the world's population, accounts for 14% of the global number of people living with HIV/AIDS and 12% of global annual AIDS deaths."

The article points the finger at leadership: "After 13 years, South Africa still does not have a comprehensive economic development plan. It has no industrial or employment strategies. There is no leadership, vision or ambition. The economy is on autopilot. There are no new ideas. The smug ruling elite is satisfied with its mediocrity. We deserve better. We cannot continue on the same path."

Leadership is the problem with South Africa's "slash-and-burn macroeconomic policy" (the title of the article by Gqubule). One day leaders will have to answer for the lives lost unnecessarily to HIV/AIDS on their watch. (Another 1 million people will die before another regime can be voted in... of what the *Economist* magazine calls "state indifference" - it is a case of sins of omission.) This will bring the total to around the 3 million mark – ten times more than the loss of life in Uganda under Amin, in roughly the same period of time.

Few would argue that Lenin and Stalin after him were strong leaders. But history has judged them not just for the blood on their hands, but because their very policies killed people. Thirty million peasants died as a result of collectivization. Yet people like George Bernard Shaw visited the Soviet Union and raved about the miracle of socialism in the media.

C4L is concerned about leadership because it is concerned about orphans and vulnerable children (OVC). They have become the living legacy of the pandemic as it enters the death phase. As C4L is not a medical mission, it found a way to engage with those who are "affected" as opposed to "infected" - although some 20% of those who have died from AIDS are children. C4L now has an innovative programme that advocates "kinship care" as opposed to "foster care". In recent years, this has come to be recognized as the state of the art in the new millennium.

As C4L explored the roots of the problem of OVC, it concluded that leadership has to be strengthened, starting with child heads of household – Africa's youngest leaders. Then community volunteers, teachers and pastors – not to mention the OVC themselves.

C4L has also realized that service provision is not enough – Christian groups have a responsibility in terms of advocacy as well. So it is becoming more vocal about what is not being done, as well as more engaged in doing what needs to be done.

A recent study by *Macleans* magazine in Canada established what is called an "admiration index". For what it's worth, it rates leaders in what is essentially an opinion poll. An Angus Reid statement said: "Politicians fare less well than activists in the rankings because they are in the business of trying to be all things to all people. Humanitarians, on the other hand, can stand up for one noble cause, and can compromise less. It found Nelson Mandela and Bill Gates to be the most esteemed leaders among the 5,800 people polled in 20 countries.

Bono and the Dalai Lama scored high on the list as well – philanthropists, artists and religious leaders.

It is critical to keep a "third sector" (i.e. neither government nor private sector) growing in Africa, and C4L is one of the few institutions that exists for that purpose alone. Some call it the "social sector" and others call it "civil society". Whatever the label, it contains the community service groups, the faith constituencies, the sports clubs, the humanitarian organizations, the arts institutions, and so on.

Leadership development at this level is critical. Not only for there to be effective and efficient service provision, but for there to be a prophetic voice to engage the powers with the same courage and wisdom with which Nathan confronted King David. Ironically, to do this well, one should not be watching an admiration index!

Another irony is that the resources to do such work often flow down from patrons in government or commerce. Suffice it to say that - contrary to popular belief - the squeaky wheels do not always get greased!

This will be the one and only appeal that C4L makes during this season of Lent. You are asked to sacrifice in any way that will affect your own values and lifestyle. This season begins with ashes, and ends with the ultimate victory.

Victory, according to John F Kennedy, has a thousand fathers... but defeat is an orphan. I'm not sure what you call a country with a burgeoning population of orphans?

He gave me beauty for ashes The oil of joy for mourning
And the garment of praise for the spirit of heaviness.

The Danger of Scapegoating

There are still many unanswered questions surrounding the outbreak of Listeriosis. The Minister of Health of South Africa has been under pressure to find the source of this pestilence and root it out. This is because of the panic that starts to rise in citizens who are familiar with the history of plagues.

The Great Plague left an indelible memory on mankind. Sometimes called the Black Death, this pestilence ravaged the whole world for 4 years. About 30% of the population of Eurasia and North Africa was decimated. India was depopulated. Mesopotamia, Syria and Armenia were covered in dead bodies. Florence lost 50 000 of its 100 000 inhabitants. England lost four out of ten citizens. Untold millions of people perished. World population did not recover to pre-plague levels for 4 centuries. Governments could do nothing to protect citizens because no one could get to the root of the problem.

Of course most people at that time still believed that the world was flat. But there were already universities graduating doctors of medicine. No one could figure it out.

Only in 1894, in another outbreak in China of this dreaded pestilence, did a Russian scientist working for the Pasteur Institute finally identify the bacterium. He had the dubious honour of having had it named after him! Only then did the domino-effect of the bubonic plague come to be understood. The bacterium is indigenous to Siberia and Mongolia. It lives naturally inside fleas that drink blood from "hosts" usually rodents (e.g. rats) or alternatively humans. Rats travel on ships laden with grain (on board the fleas bite sailors too). So ships from strategic sea ports in the Grain Trade carried the pestilence from port to port. Sailors and rats interacted with city folk, spreading the infection. Thence it spread around the world.

The scapegoating in this instance was that Europeans turned on the Jews in racist fury. They said they suspected the Jews of poisoning wells. As this race dressed differently, due to its religious customs, it was identifiable. Pogroms began – especially in Germany. Long before Hitler, anti-Semitism reared its ugly head. People get scared silly by pestilence.

Citizens in South Africa are caught between two forces today – the right to know, and the lack of definitive proof. Already some companies like Tiger Brands and Rainbow have been named. The share price of these companies has crashed as a result of a proactive recall of suspected meat products. But the companies are not apologizing yet...

Only a century ago, in 1917, came another unexpected pestilence – the Flu Epidemic. Comparing the Spanish Flu, as it came to be known... three times more people died of the influenza epidemic than died in combat in World War I which was raging at the time. Within a few months, a third of the global population came down with the virus. In India it killed 5 per cent of the population (15 million people). On the island of Tahiti, 14 per cent died. On Samoa, 20 per cent. In the copper mines of the Congo one out of five labourers perished.

Altogether the pandemic killed between 50 million and 100 million people in less than a year. World War I killed 40 million over four years.

There was a reverse feature of this strain of flu virus. Usually the most vulnerable to influenza are children, the elderly and the weak. But this strain took out healthy adults – like soldiers. Nearly half of the population aged 20 – 40 in the USA perished – a disproportionately high rate by age bracket. Life expectancy in the USA dropped by 12 years! Native American tribes were particularly hard hit.

No one really knows for sure where it started (possibly in Kansas?), nor can anyone explain why it ended so abruptly – about two weeks after the second surge peaked in late 1918. So the scapegoating began... one conspiracy theory emerged that Big Pharma was behind this epidemic. This narrative is that it had produced a flu vaccine and wanted to cash in on the profits before the war ended. So it mobilized mass vaccination of both troops and civilians. Not just in the USA but in other countries. Soldiers started dying in the USA before there were ever deployed to the front in Europe. Some countries like Greece declined the vaccines and were not devastated by the epidemic.

The outbreak of Listeriosis in 2017 has brought such scenarios to people's minds. Of course there have been huge advances in medical science and technology, but for a year now the researchers have been stumped. The rather abrupt announcement that a culprit has been found raises some eyebrows in a country where there is no shortage of conspiracy theories – from the recurring "third force" to allegations of "regime change" agendas. The Department of Health has to provide scientific proof of its finger-pointing, according to the CEO of Tiger Brands.

Then in the 1980s another pestilence appeared. South Africa is now at the eye of this storm, in terms of its prevalence, of this AIDS pandemic. Close to 15 percent of its citizens are now HIV-positive. Other countries like China and India may have more infected people in absolute terms? But as their base populations are so huge by comparison, it is a relatively low infection *rate*.

This is also classified as a "sexually-transmitted disease" although there are other ways that it can be contracted. Thus there is a double-jeopardy involved - called Stigma. This has its roots in the images of pandemics past, where just getting infected was a death sentence.

Not to mention that it is an STD with all the connotations that this term can bring to mind. AIDS was a very devious disease. Unlike the bubonic plague or the Spanish flu, those infected could not detect it right away. Furthermore, this HIV virus itself is not the killer. Instead, it compromises the body's immune system, so the victims die of "opportunistic infections". This is one reason that you rarely heard of people "dying of AIDS" – the other reason was Stigma.

This made it very difficult to track down the root of the pestilence. But within 2 years medical science had identified it, and within 10 years, treatment was available. Meanwhile, to date, 30 million people have died of this pandemic. Tens of millions of others have either been "infected" (i.e. they are now HIV-positive) or "affected" (e.g. the "deluge of orphans" as Dr Stephen Lewis once put it in his aptly-titled book Race Against Time).

Again there was scapegoating. Some nasty conspiracy theories emerged around the AIDS pandemic. They never did find "Patient Zero"... but the Science Museum's History of Medicine website includes a section titled "*The fault of others: exiles, scapegoats and the human face of disease.*" It describes the tendency throughout history to target marginal groups, minorities, and the poor as scapegoats for plagues and diseases. It was a means to allay fears and reinforce prejudices. Examples cited include the Black Death that was blamed on Jews and cholera on immigrant Irish workers. Syphilis was called "the

French Disease" in England, and the French in turn blamed the Italians who in turn blamed the French.

In fact, AIDS involves multiple epidemics. As well as an epidemic of HIV, we experienced epidemics of fear and of stigmatization, scapegoating and discrimination. These are associated with any pestilence in general and with AIDS in particular. In order to deal humanely and compassionately with AIDS and persons living with HIV and AIDS – and to protect society (including the fundamental principles and rules on which it is based) - a primary requirement is to recognize that *we are all living with AIDS*, whether infected by it, affected by it or at risk. That is, in the context of AIDS, it is imperative that we overcome any divisions into 'them' and 'us'.

Dealing with plagues and pestilence is never easy – either from the medical or the social point of view. The Department of Health needs to provide conclusive proof of its findings.

Companies have suffered reputation loss, there could be significant job losses, and investors have taken a hit.

But of course, the paramount concern is that 181 lives have been lost. Above all, their families and loved ones are the ones who need answers. Real answers, not conspiracy theories.

6. THE HARBINGER

John Wycliffe

The holy man's only possession is his begging bowl

A new word entered my vocabulary this week, reading an autobiography of John Wycliffe – "simony". He used the word quite a bit to describe those who were ultimately in ministry for their own benefit, not for the sake of any "beneficiaries". As an academic, in a church that was ensconced in politics, Wycliffe railed against many issues. One was the buying and selling of church offices – in other words you could pay to become a bishop, or if you could afford it, to become a cardinal. This was one of various fundraising strategies that led Rome astray – another one is better known because of Martin Luther's critique – that is, the buying and selling of indulgences. Fifty years before Luther, in Britain not Germany, Wycliffe preached against those too.

Observers noted that Wycliffe's personal austerity authenticated his ministry as an Oxford academic and the "morning star" of the Protestant Reformation. One of his foreign students at Oxford was a man named John Hus from Bohemia – who was also, later, branded a heretic by Rome. First Wycliffe, then Hus, then Luther.

In an earlier wave of reform, St Francis of Assisi and Dominic de Guzman had launched the Franciscan and Dominican orders respectively in Italy and Spain. Their "friars" operated in the monastic movement, in parallel to the church hierarchy of priests, prelates, bishops, cardinals and popes. I say popes (plural) because during Wycliffe's lifetime, there were periods when there was more than one pope – sometimes two and in efforts to mediate a return to one, at times a third was elected. It was mayhem! Popes were sometimes military men, and always wealthy. In fact, only an emperor could be regarded at pope level – above kings.

But there were movements like these – including the Lollards that Wycliffe launched - who adopted that "back to the future" policy that came to be known as the separation of church and state. Wycliffe was very strong on this, and probably more than anything, that is what brought down the wrath of his Archbishop of Canterbury on him and his followers.

To digress, we get previous glimpses of asceticism far back into church history – the desert fathers for example, who emulated John the Baptist for centuries. The early church seems to have held worldly wealth in relatively low esteem – the haves selling off assets to provide for the needs of the have-nots. Before the church was "un-banned" by Constantine, it had come to be known as the "Third Way". Not the Roman way of Power; not the Jewish way of Wealth; but rather the third way of Love. Christian service.

Then came the "decriminalization" of Christianity and over the centuries, the fusion (and confusion!) caused by merger of church and state. "The Holy Roman Empire". When the French invaded Britain in 1066 they were the ascendant power in Europe. By the 14th century, they even decided they should re-locate the Papacy to Avingon, lest there be "two centres of power". It was during this period that Wycliffe arose and his sharp mind saw through this nonsense.

Wycliffe saw one thing very clearly – the Bible everyone used at the time was the Latin Vulgate. It was not the original Hebrew *old testament* or Greek Septuagint (OT translated into Greek from Hebrew by 72 scholars, from whence comes its name). Neither was it the original Greek *new testament*. It was a translation – done by St Jerome. But it was treated as God's infallible Word at a time when literacy was low, giving the Clergy hegemony over the Laity. He saw that lay people outnumbered the clergy – even though there were local priests and itinerant friars all over the place (much more ubiquitous than in today's world). So he sensed that the "balance of powers" in terms of the policy debates that raged in academia (at his level) would be tipped if an English translation of the whole Bible existed.

Even though he himself was very good at translating, he was just too busy to do it. So he got a team going, which grew into a movement called the Lollards. I myself had not realized that his translation was a team effort – like the Septuagint had been, in Antioch, and other future translations would be too (like the King James Version). He did not translate scripture into English himself – the way Martin Luther did into German. It was a systematic team effort. Strategically linked to his "public engagement" ministry.

Nor was it done in academic isolation, for its own sake. Wycliffe set about it intentionally to off-set the advantage that the Clergy always had over the Laity. And there was value-added to that, because of three the roots of English in Old German, Old Slavic and French (reflecting successive invasions of England). Translating the Bible helped the language to "gel" instead of there being different creoles in different parts of the Isle. And this had a huge influence on nationalism – an important factor when a later King decided to stand up against Rome.

Wycliffe admired the "spiritual Franciscans" – the branch of that order that taught that the church should not own private property. They believed that the state owned the land, and the monarch sub-divided it among feudal lords in the aristocracy. He railed against church leaders holding public office, and felt that the church should rather *speak truth to power*, as we would say today. For this reason he was often more disliked by senior church officials than by the government! Although the two of these were by now so entangled that they closed ranks against him and forced the Lollards "underground". Still it thrived, and largely because the Bible had been fully translated into English by then.

However, the printing press had not been invented yet, at this time. Manuscripts were still copied by hand – a labour intensive technology. Fortunately, this could be done relatively inconspicuously, in the parlours of manor homes in deep rural areas. So it was very hard for government to put an end to it.

The same is true of the "begging friars". Like the Lollards, they moved around rural areas quite freely. The Lollards preached from an English Bible and espoused the views of Wycliffe - which even went so far as to disagree with the relatively recent doctrine of Transubstantiation. Wycliffe knew from research that early church fathers like Tertullian and Augustine did not believe in this. But Tradition had come to be more influential than Scripture, so for this, the Lollards were despised by the Roman Catholic church.

At this stage, the Roman church had replaced the earlier models of Christianity in England and Ireland. It was not the first. In fact, one mission was founded by hermits at Glastonbury, before there was a church in Rome. Tertullian referred to Britain as a Christian nation and the British Church was recognized by the Council of Arles in 314, only one year after Christianity was decriminalized by Constantine. By 432, St Patrick had gone to evangelize Ireland, whose peregrini missionaries had later rebounded to Britain and mainland Europe. This was over a century before Augustine of Canterbury came to evangelize Britain with Roman Catholicism in 597.

So when the Protestant Reformation rebounded into Britain from the Europe of Luther and Calvin, it found a very fertile context which quickly embraced reform. The famous Via Media was adopted.

What really stands out to me is the authenticity that comes from the ministry of "poor friars" whose life-style validates that they are not in it for themselves, like Simon Magus, from whom the term "simony" derives. Wycliffe personified this image of one who denied himself to validate his ministry of speaking truth to power.

But I have to add that all these mendicant friars and their orders only survive through the generosity of ordinary parishioners and wealthy donors. Sometimes these are well-to-do women like the ones who financed Jesus and his ministry. Sometimes there is a very public response like the city slickers who flocked down to the Jordan River to be baptized by John, the greatest of all prophets according to Jesus. Or those who flocked to hear the late, great Billy Graham preach – like in Los Angeles in the early 1950s. That outreach changed the course of a mega-city's history. For without personal renewal there cannot be social renewal.

Like the mendicant orders and the Lollards, the modern missionary movement could never have functioned without support of "home churches". Likewise, philanthropy evolved into NGOs that are supported by many donations, not just the Foundations of the vastly wealthy like Carnegie and Gates. As Palm Sunday approaches... those of you who can, are encouraged to give *generously*. Just as those of us whose gift is mercy must do it *cheerfully*. (Romans 12).

7. RADICAL REFORMERS

Erasmus

Ramaphosa is more like Erasmus that Martin Luther

The Protestant Reformation is seen by some as the rebirth of a corrupted Christianity, and by others as the departure of a mistaken minority, who over time came to outnumber Catholics as they do today. Luther was not the most radical of the Reformers, but he is probably the best known.

But it was the earlier work of Erasmus that unleashed Luther to write his 95 Theses and post them on the Wittenburg door. Erasmus was one of the dominant figures of the early humanist movement, who never joined the Reform movement and remained a Catholic for all of his life.

Erasmus was neither a radical Reformer nor an apologist for the status quo. It was his publication of a Greek New Testament, laden with his comments and questions, that brought on a theological revolution. Then later, his views on the Reformation tempered its more radical elements.

African radicals are likely to protest that this comparison is already Euro-centric, but I plead that the Northern Europe of 1516 when Erasmus published his Greek New Testament and of 1517 when Luther posted his 95 Theses on the church door, was not guilty of colonialism. In fact, nation-states did not really exist yet, they were just forming as the peoples of Northern Europe tried to shake off the yoke of Rome's oppression. Rome asserted its hegemony largely through church structures, which drew from the deep well of Christian beliefs and convictions. So Christianity unified Europe, and Latin was still the lingua franca where ever you went (not English!).

The history of Capetown is instructive. What Portugal had been seeking was another route to the Orient. It was in 1488 that Bartholemeu Dias first rounded the Horn, which was long before the

Dutch sent van Riebeek to set up Capetown. And at first that port was more of a supply stop en route to the Orient than a colony.

The initial aspirations were not so much for Colonialism as for an alternative trade route. This is because Constantinople had fallen to the Ottoman Turks in 1453, putting a strangle- hold on the Silk Route to the Orient. The "Reconquista" of Granada was only finished in 1492, so even the Spanish were not dreaming of a New World when they commissioned Columbus.

He was from Genoa, the centre of trade with Constantinople, and knew how important this alternative trade route aspiration was to Portugal and Spain. He tried first to get the Portuguese to finance his "sail West" project, but they were succeeding with the Horn of

Africa route so they didn't see the point. So he went to Spain where King Ferdinand and Queen Isabella decided to finance his venture. Remember there was little inkling that the Americas were even there to colonize, when Columbus set sail in 1492. He first landed at the Bahamas, then Dominican Republic... still thinking he was almost at Japan.

Cortez did not invade Mexico until 1519. Pizarro invaded the Inca kingdom about 20 years after that. So I think that one can justifiably excuse the Northern Europe of Erasmus and Luther from a Colonial agenda. Cromwell didn't even invade Ireland until 1649! That was England's first colonial project.

At the age of 17, in 1483, Erasmus lost both his parents to the Black Death. In 1492 – the same year that Columbus discovered the "Indies" (which turned out not to be the East as he thought it was) – poverty forced Erasmus into monastery life and he was ordained a Catholic priest, but it seems that he never actively worked as a cleric.

Erasmus's life changed dramatically when he became secretary for Henry de Bergen, bishop of Chambray, who was impressed with his skill in Latin. The bishop enabled Erasmus to travel to Paris, France, to study classical literature and Latin, and it was there that he was introduced to Renaissance humanism. While in Paris, Erasmus became known as an excellent scholar and lecturer. One of his pupils, William Blunt, Lord Montjoy, established a pension for Erasmus, allowing him to adopt a life of an independent scholar moving from city to city tutoring, lecturing and corresponding with some of the most brilliant thinkers of Europe. He met great minds like Thomas More and John Colet, and moved between France, the Netherlands and England, writing some of his best works.

His translation of the New Testament into Greek in 1516 was a turning point in theology and the interpretation of scripture, and posed a serious challenge to theological thinking that had dominated universities since they first emerged. Erasmus promoted the spread of classical knowledge to encourage a better morality, good governance and greater understanding between people.

St Jerome's "Vulgate" was regarded as the Word of God. But it was only a translation into "vulgar" (meaning everyday) Latin as opposed to the "high" Latin of Cicero and Julius Caesar. Erasmus saw through this, and knew that by publishing a Greek New Testament with a lot of probing questions, he would be able to provoke debate and thus (he hoped) cause a cleansing of church corruption and oppression.

Only about 50 years earlier, Guttenberg had invented the printing press. So Erasmus was using the cutting edge of technology to provoke debate and reform.

But the Protestant Reformation only erupted with the publication of Martin Luther's Ninety- five Theses in 1517. For the next decade, Erasmus would be embroiled in an intellectual debate. Though he supported Protestant ideals, he was against the radicalism of some of its leaders, and even condemned Luther's methods.

Luther later (in hiding because of the political upheaval) translated the New Testament into German. His translation had a defining effect on the emergence of Germany as a nation.

Just as the translation much later of the Bible into Afrikaans had a defining effect on the "white tribe of Africa".

It seems that by disposition, and perhaps because the recently elected Top Six is "split" with the Zuma faction, President Ramaphosa is more of an Erasmus that a Martin Luther. It seems that he proceeds too cautiously to really take on the challenge. He does not seem to have the "fire in the belly" of a die-hard Reformer.

Certainly his arrival is most welcome, and a harbinger of change. But as Luther was to find out, the status quo will not go down without a fight. Rome was adamant that Reformers like Luther should recant of their views, and it continued to insist that its ways were justified.

"Zexit" (Zuma's exit) is hopefully not just the departure of one leader, but of the Way of Leading that he has championed. It has been called "Triumphalism" because its proponents behaved arrogantly, as if they would always remain in power, and thus were accountable to no one. It sounds like Rome around 1500, raising funds to finance the Vatican by selling indulgences.

Erasmus tackled that triumphalism as a scholar and his Greek New Testament and probing questions certainly shook Rome's foundations. But he did not get militant like Luther and the other real Reformers. Although it is interesting to see that Humanism – which Erasmus was one of the first to articulate – has given Christianity (both Catholic and Protestant together) a run for its money ever since!

My observation is that Luther the premiere Reformer had not yet emerged at the time that Erasmus started his probing. I think that a new leader will soon emerge in South Africa who will eclipse Ramaphosa too. Even though I admire what Ramaphosa is doing, to get rid of Zuma and Triumphalism. President Ramaphosa seems to have the temperament of an Erasmus, not of a Luther.

Last year the Save South Africa movement emerged. Currently there is the #ZumaMustGo movement. There are numerous opposition parties vying for Reform. Organized labour is split into factions, some pro-Zuma, some anti-Zuma.

There are a number of rising stars – among them Maimane, Malema, Vavi, Mapaila, Khoza – who are relatively young and bright. They are the Luther, Calvin, Simmons, and Cramner of our time. This is a Reformation of those who jointly protest against Triumphalist corruption and malpractice. It is a democratic movement and it is likely to make President Ramaphosa an important but moderate Reformer – not a radical. Like Erasmus. This is still a huge compliment.

It is also a rebuke to the Zuma loyalists who remain. Just like Saddam Hussein lighting the oil wells on fire as he retreated out of Kuwait, Zuma has left a legacy in the NPA and the Public Protector. Even in the Top Six. Thank God that the Triumphalists efforts to corrupt the Judiciary failed, that is what saved South Africa.

Erasmus would advise us to go back to the classics – the Constitution, the Freedom Charter, and to correct the course that led us astray. Don't look at the vulgar interpretation of these document, look again at the originals. Ask impertinent questions. Challenge authority. And reform...

Martin Luther

Martin Luther got irritated enough at the way things were being done by the church, that he dared to post a list of 95 theses on the door of the church at Wittenberg. His list caused quite a stir.

So he was summoned to Worms in an effort to get him to recant his views. That is where he is reputed to have said, "Here I stand, I can do no other."

Neither the 95 theses nor the Diet of Worms that followed can be said to have been the starting point of the Reformation. The really came at another event that occurred under a tree outside the wall of Wittenberg. This place was a sort of incinerator – when unclean things were burned, for hygienic purposes. Symbolically, Luther took the papal bull – a kind of arrest warrant – out of the city to that place, and burned it. To make the point that it was unclean.

During apartheid in South Africa, blacks had to carry a passbook if they had any reason to walk through an area zoned for whites. Symbolically, some leaders of the struggle took their passbooks outside and publicly burned them. Signifiying that they were unjust.

So in both North and South, similar strategies have been used to ignite change processes.

Bob Geldorf sums up the global need for change by saying that there must be a new social contract between North and South, guaranteeing more:

From the North (DAT) From the South (DAT)

Debt relief	Democracy
Aid	Accountability
Trade	Transparency

Along these lines, we have prepared a new 95 theses for change. These address issues related to the people, organizations and institutions that say they want to convert, transform, change, renew, regenerate, reconstruct, uplift, etc.

If you want to change others, first change yourself, is a saying that Alcoholics Anonymous, a well-respected change agent, has taught many people.

These 95 theses come at issues from both directions at once. They challenge actors of both North and South. They try to offend all of these equally!

The Divine Right of Parties

In his book <u>Wide as the Waters</u>, Benson Bobrick tracks "the story of the English Bible *and the revolution it inspired*." He writes a painstaking history from before the Protestant Reformation (Wycliffe) on. Through the plethora of Bible translations that emerged from the diverse strains of the Reformation, on to the "Authorized Version". This was not only a great version in technical terms, but an effort to synthesize previous work and thus find a Via Media between the Catholic counter-reformation on the conservative side, and the Non-conformists on the radical side.

The struggle between the "divine right of kings" and emerging Democracy is ever-present. Certainly the emergence of nation-states like Germany had made it possible for Martin Luther to translate Scripture into the vernacular. Conversely, his translation had the symbiotic effect of unifying the language.

Centuries later, the same thing happened with Afrikaans in South Africa. It was really a "creole" mixing Dutch, French, Portuguese, and local terms until the Bible was translated. Over a period of several decades, this hardened the creole into what is now the youngest language in the world. The Afrikaans Bible Museum in Paarl captures this more recent story.

In England, King James I, who authorized the "King James Version" had Non-conformist inclinations, deriving from his earlier years as king of Scotland. When Elizabeth I died, she being a royalist as well insisted that he was the legitimate heir to the throne. But he embraced the Via Media which Elizabeth I's long reign had embedded in British life, following her father Henry VIII's "nationalization" of the church. At first this was for his own private reasons, but it aligned with the Protestant Reformation and thus Bible translation was suddenly encouraged instead of outlawed.

There were too many swings of the pendulum to relate here. Some monarchs brutally reinstated Catholicism, others endorsed the Via Media, and some made more space for the Non-conformists. Some writers at the time compared this to the stories of good kings and bad kings recorded in the two Books of Kings in the Old Testament.

The real show-down came when Charles I ascended to the throne and tried to re-assert Catholicism. Over a decade passed without the king convening Parliament. But by this time, the combined inertia of the Via Media and the Non-conformists was just too great. So they both eventually raised armies, and England plunged into all-out Civil War.

The monarch was defeated – and beheaded. Oliver Cromwell emerged as Lord Protector of a republican government. For three generations, England tried to make it without a monarch. This even took martial law at times. But alas. Again, the inertia of the Via Media was just too great, and Bobrick attributes this to the fact that the population had become "People of the Book". To be British was neither Catholic nor radical Non-conformist, it was the Via Media than combines them both. So the monarchy was reinstated under Charles II who was foolish enough to try to bring back Catholicism! The backlash was to invite William of orange to come over from the Low Countries, for he was married to a legitimate heir to the British crown. His armies landed and made short work of it.

But when he arrived in London, to popular acclaim, he refused to accept the crown by virtue of military victory. Instead, he insisted on Parliament being convened and inviting him to be monarch. The rapprochement of that moment has remained in place ever since. Of course Parliament has gained strength as Democracy matured, and kings have become but figureheads. But this synthesis can be traced back to the Protestant Reformation rejecting the authority of Rome, and to the translation of Scripture - that liberated the laity.

The Seeds of Revolution

During this period of foment in Britain, two other things were happening. First, the Age of Exploration had passed (it was roughly concurrent with the Protestant Reformation) and Colonization had begun. Especially in North America, across the Atlantic from Britain, the 13 colonies were beginning to gel. Many of these were populated by radical Non-conformists, who noted that even Britain had rejected the monarchy for a protracted period. Only one of these (Maryland) was founded on Catholicism, although in South America it was a different story. The mainly Spanish colonies were very Catholic.

(Let's remember that the Cape Colony was established by the Dutch, which had liberated themselves from Spanish hegemony and where Non-conformist doctrines were also paramount. This DNA passed on to the settlers in South Africa, which included the Heugenots – basically the Protestant refugees run out of France by the Catholic counter- reformation.)

Second, philosophy was being influenced by the likes of John Locke and Thomas Hobbes who were moving political science onto new horizons. Their thinking greatly influenced American thinkers like Thomas Jefferson, who drafted both the Declaration of Independence and the American Constitution.

This was a huge example of an Ocean Bridge. To a limited extent, political theory was secularizing. Humanism was emerging from its roots in Christianity. Even Erasmus, one of the first Bible translators, who influenced Martin Luther, is remembered as one of the earliest Humanists, in the earliest stages of the Protestant Reformation. But now the radical rejection of Rome's authority was coming home to roost. The words of the king who remarked "No bishop, no king" had become prophetic.

This Ocean Bridge was crossed (from the Old World to the New World) by four fundamental new cornerstones:

1. *Self-evident laws of nature* – reason and conscience were replacing theology as the foundations for rights, justice and Democracy
2. *Common law* – While the debate about the authority of Scripture (Protestants) versus Tradition (Catholics) was on-going, Law evolved a way of practicing a respect for previous decisions
3. *Separation of church and state* – with religious tolerance came space for pluralism and the fight against bigotry and xenophobia evolved a "melting pot" approach to immigration

4. *Classless egalitarianism* – America rejected both the monarchy and the aristocracy and adopted the notion that all men are created equal. This was rotted in the *Imago Dei*

The American Revolution of course resulted in a formalized social contract: "We the people..."

To quote Broderick: "As long as Scripture could mean as many different things to as many people as read it, the deeply thought-through conclusions of the Church down through the ages were allowed no more stature than the cloudy revelations of individual minds. And insofar as those revelations prompted actions, chaos might result. No democracy, in fact, could fail to destroy itself without some restraint imposed upon liberty – as governing action – in this sense. There had to be a frame. The great unwritten Constitution of England, and the arguably greater Constitution of the United States, with its Bill of Rights, took the theological place in Civil Society of the Received Wisdom laid down by the Church councils and preserved in Creeds.

Then this new commitment to life, liberty and property crossed the Ocean Bridge again. Americans assisted to the French Revolution and received a gift from France thereafter – the Statue of Liberty.

The Shift of Focus to Free and Fair Elections

This revolution kept eroding at the ever-evolving status quo. The Anti-Slavery Movement, the Suffragettes, the Liberation Struggle against Colonialism, the Universal Declaration of Human Rights, the Civil Rights Movement, and the latest push for LGBTI+ rights can all be seen as chapters of Democratization.

This Ocean Bridge brought change to African colonies as well. The Union of South Africa was the first nation on the continent to gain independence, but it was only the European men who then ruled. Racial and gender equality followed slowly. At first only white men voted. Later in the era of apartheid came a Tri-cameral Parliament. Finally to be replaced with free and fair elections in 1994.

Democracy has evolved from a confrontation with the "divine right of kings" to a Party system, with so much focus in electioneering. As the executive power of kings faded (except in eSwatini, of course), the focus of Democracy changed to *elections*. Although Democracy is much more than that, it has come to be defined as that.

The "look and feel" of George Washington was not unlike that of an executive monarch. The party system has not yet evolved. That would come a generation later in the huge debates between Thomas Jefferson and Alexander Hamilton. Before long you had Republicans contesting elections with Democrats. But only men were voting still. The suffrage was not universal.

In Britain the contest was between the Conservatives and the Liberals, as the monarchy waned in terms of executive power. Parliaments and Prime Ministers squeezed the royals out of executive power. However, the House of Lords retains some power for the aristocracy. But the House of Commons reflects the engagement of all citizens, and is where the real power lies.

On the other side of the Ocean Bridge, in the republican USA, there are also two Houses in Parliament – the Congress and the Senate. But as a class system did not really exist, this dichotomy does another balancing act – between proportional representation and equality of all the states. It is hard to imagine Rhode Island and Texas on a par, but the Senate helps to level out that disparity. Whereas high density urban areas can elect more Congressmen (and now Congresswomen) that sparsely populated states "out west".

The Electoral College" system in America was introduced to try to further level the playing field. But in the elections of John Kennedy, George W Bush and Donald Trump, the elections were extremely close. It is possible to win without getting a majority vote in this curious electoral arrangement.

To date, no woman has been elected President of the USA. Maggie Thatcher was the first woman in Britain to become Prime Minister.

Barrack Obama was the first African American to be elected President. But what really marked a historical change was when Nelson Mandela was elected President of South Africa.

Elections everywhere now require independent "observers" to validate that they are free and fair. This is the new focus of Democracy, perhaps to the detriment of the other institutions that keep Democracy from falling apart – like the Judiciary, the other levels of government (provincial, state, municipal), the Media and Civil Society.

Across this Ocean Bridge, many key people and ideas have crossed back and forth. The inter-change of ideas keeps evolving Democracy and its focus.

Democracy needs to sink into organizations and families as well. Bishops can be despots and fathers can be abusive. Decision-making at all levels of society needs to be inclusive and participative. It has often been said that "a family that prays together stays together". Certainly, biblical literacy can do no harm and could do a lot of good. Reformation doctrines like "the priesthood of all believers" have shaken authority and challenged bishops, kings, parliaments and families to involve all those who are affected by a decision in the process of decision making. That is probably the essence of Democracy and in our Open Society the Ocean Bridge has been widened.

8. THE AGE OF DISCOVERY AND COLONIALISM

Krotoa

"Humans being humans and sex being sex, that prohibition never stopped anyone. There were mixed kids in South Africa nine months after the first Dutch boats hit the beach in Table Bay." (Trevor Noah)

With a little help from Wikipedia, I captured and re-jigged the following sketch of "the mother of our nation"...

Krotoa (or **Eva**) was born in 1643. This was 9 years before the Dutch arrived to establish the Cape Colony. 155 years had passed since Bartholomeu Dias first circumvented the Cape of Good Hope, in the early days in the Age of Discovery. So for over a century, this sea-route to the Orient was being used. The Dutch finally decided to establish a permanent stop-over point for provisioning at what is now Cape Town.

Slave trading had already begun in West Africa by the time of Krotoa's birth – but that coast was much closer to America and the Caribbean. It would still be a century before the Abolitionists emerged, and 152 years before the London Missionary Society was founded in tandem to that. Meanwhile, the focus of the sea expeditions to the Orient was still exploration and trade. Only after the LMS got into gear would that narrow focus expand to include philanthropy, development and empowerment.

Krotoa was born as a member of the Goringhaicona or Strandlopers tribe. They were sedentary, non-pastoral hunter-gathers. They are believed to be one of the first clans to make acquaintances with the Dutch people. She was the niece of a Khoi leader and trader called Autshumato. Her uncle was a clan leader and Krotoa's fate and fortunes were closely aligned to his. Prior to the Dutch's arrival Autshumato served as a postal agent for passing ships of a number of countries.

Circumstantial evidence suggests that at the time of the arrival of the Dutch, Krotoa lived with her uncle Autshumato (also known as Harry by the Dutch). At the age of 11 or 12 she was taken in to work in the household of Jan van Riebeeck, the first governor of the Cape Colony. There are multiple accounts of how Krotoa came to work under the household of Jan Van Riebeeck. One account paints the story of how the Dutch forcefully kidnapped the child Krotoa, however no hard evidence confirms this account. Krotoa was taken in as a companion and as a servant to Riebeeck's wife and children.

If the theory of Krotoa having lived with her uncle is true, then Krotoa's early service to the Dutch may not have been as violent a transition as it is sometimes made out to be. It is believed that the first baby born to chaplain/sick-healer Willem Barentssen Wijlant and his wife - coupled with the rapid spreading of a virulent disease in the settlement - sparked the initial negotiations to obtain services from a local girl. As Autshumato had a long history of working for Europeans, it is believed that the Dutch first turned to Autshumato for negotiations. It is quite possible that Autshumato offered up his niece for servitude in order to better his standings with the Dutch.

Many authors and historians speculate that she might have become a teenage mistress of Van Riebeek, based on the fondness presented towards her in his journals.

So as a teenager, she learned Dutch, Portuguese and French, and like her uncle, worked as an interpreter for the Dutch who wanted to trade goods for cattle. Unlike her uncle however, Krotoa was able to obtain a higher position within the Dutch hierarchy as she additionally served as a trading agent, an ambassador for a high ranking chief and a peace negotiator in time of war. Her story exemplifies the initial dependency of the Dutch newcomers on the natives who were able to provide reasonably reliable information about the local inhabitants.

On 3 May 1662 – when she was 19 years old - she was baptized by a visiting parson, minister Petrus Sibelius, in the church inside the Fort de Goede Hoop. The witnesses were Roelof de Man and Pieter van der Stael.

On 26 April 1664 – at age 21 - she married a Danish surgeon by the name of Peter Havgard, whom the Dutch called Pieter van Meerhof. She was thereafter known as Eva van Meerhof. She was the first Khoikoi to marry according to Christian customs. There was a little party in the house of Zacharias Wagenaer.

In May 1665, van Meerhof was appointed superintendent of Robben Island, so they left Cape Town. The family briefly returned to the mainland in 1666 after the birth of Krotoa's third child, in order to baptize the baby. Van Meerhoff was murdered on an expedition to Madagascar on 27 February 1668.

After the death of her husband came the appointment of a new governor - Zacharias Wagenaer. Unlike the governor before him he held extremely negative views toward the Khoi people and because at this point the Dutch settlement was secure, he didn't find a need for Krotoa as a translator anymore.

So the widow Krotoa returned to the mainland on 30 September 1668 with her children - unemployed. Suffering from alcoholism, in her late twenties, she left the Castle in the settlement to be with her family in the kraals. In February 1669 she was imprisoned unjustly for immoral behavior at the Castle and then banished to Robben Island. One of Van

Riebeeck's nieces, Elizabeth Van Opdorp, adopted Krotoa's children after she was banished.

She returned to the mainland more than once just to find herself banished to Robben Island again. In May 1673 she was allowed to baptise another child on the mainland. Only three of her children survived infancy. The two of these who were fathered by Van Meerhof later moved on to Mauritius with their adopted family.

Krotoa died on 29 July 1674 and was buried on 30 September 1674 in the church in the Fort. She was only 32 years old. She is noted as one of the most written about women in South African history, with her name appearing in the journals of the Dutch East India company from as early as 1652.

Her Legacy

After her death, Krotoa's story would not be deeply explored for nearly two and a half centuries. Instead attention was mostly put on white European women who came to South Africa on missionary expeditions. It was not until after the 1920s that her story become a part of South African history.

The novel *Eilande* by Dan Sleigh (1938), translated from Afrikaans by Andre Brink (in Dutch: Stemmen uit zee/in English: Islands), describes the lives of Krotoa and her daughter Pieternella from the viewpoints of seven men who knew them.

As late as 1983, under the name of Eva, she was still known in South Africa, as a caution against miscegenation.

In 1990, South African poet and author Karen Press wrote a poem entitled *Krotoa's Story* that attempted to reimagine Krotoa's life, emotions, and conflicting desires partly from her perspective. The poem was based on an earlier children's story by Press entitled *Krotoa*, which was created as part of an educational initiative by the South African Council for Higher Education designed to inform schoolchildren about colonization from the perspective of indigenous South Africans.

In 1995, South African performer Antoinette Pienaar created a one-woman play entitled *Krotoa*. The work was first performed at the Little Karoo National Arts Festival, where it was awarded the "Herrie" prize. The play is unique in its depiction and memorialization of Krotoa as a mother to the nation, a symbolization which had been previously rejected by white South Africans.

In her essay "Malintzin, Pocahontas, and Krotoa: Indigenous Women and Myth Models of the Atlantic World", University of Michigan professor Pamela Scully compared Krotoa to Malintzin and

Pocahontas, two other women of the same time period that were born in different areas of the world (Malintzin in Mesoamerica, Pocahontas in colonial Virginia). Scully argues that all three of these women had very similar experiences in the colonialist system despite being born in different regions. She reflects on the stories of Malintzin, Pocahontas, and Krotoa and states that they are almost too familiar and resonate so comfortably with a kind of inevitability and truth that seems, on reflection, perhaps too neat. Therefore, she claims, Krotoa is one of the women that can be used to show the universality of the way that people were treated in the colonial system worldwide.

Most recently of all, the full-length feature film *Krotoa* is a made-in-South-Africa motion picture, released in 2017. Its slogan is "caught between two cultures about to collide".

Relevance

Krotoa's life story should be as inspiring to missionaries as it is to women!

For the initial arrival of the Dutch in April 1652 was not unilaterally viewed as negative. Many Khoi people saw their landing as an opportunity for personal gain as middle men in the livestock trade; others saw them as potential allies against pre-existing enemies. At the peak of Krotoa's career as an interpreter, she held the belief that the Dutch presence could reap benefits on both sides.

It is not fair to always characterize indigenous people as seduced or coerced; and the arrival of foreigners as the prelude to "cultural genocide". For example, there is circumstantial evidence that Krotoa showed consistent hostility to the Goringhaiqua clan and even to her own mother, who lived with them. So why can't people – *for their reasons* – choose the approach they prefer?

Clearly, in some settings, this choice was the rejection of any foreign interference. But in Krotoa's case, one can note:

- She learned three foreign languages (Dutch, Portuguese and

French)
- She converted to Christian faith (she was baptized, and she also baptized her children. She was also buried in a church.)
- She married a white settler (and had perhaps the first "Cape Coloured" children?)
- She chose to remain in South Africa, not to emigrate
- She kept in touch with her roots
- She had a career (other than the sedentary hunting and gathering of her clan of origin)

The alcoholism that she suffered from is so, so sad, and yet so predictive. In her life, there were periods of stable marriage and parenting, as well as periods of what used to be called "back-sliding". In short, she was human. Four centuries later, the abuse of substances is still all too common among youth. We should be learning from this! So is it wise to now legalize dagga?

I take heart to learn of Krotoa's life story. Life was both good to her, and hard on her. At the end of the game, we should be congratulated for *playing well*, more than for winning.

I salute you, Krotoa, mother of our nation! Almost 400 year later, white men still find black women to be attractive, and yet we still find it hard to find one another deeply. Neither are all of us like Zacharias Wagenaer, rest assured.

Long live the black Queen!

The Modern Missionary Movement

After the Protestant Reformation in Europe came the Counter-Reformation. One of its features was the ambitious missionary work of orders like the Jesuits, in a wave that went all around the world. This was during the Age of Discovery when missionaries could travel to "the West" across the Atlantic, or around the Cape of Good Hope to "the East" namely the ports of call - all over the Indian Ocean and Pacific rim.

In tandem with the Anti-Slavery Movement a new wave of missionary activity arose out of England first and later America. Some shakers and movers in British Parliament were involved in both the Anti-Slavery and the Missionary endeavours, notably the MP William Wilberforce.

For the first time, an inter-denominational agency was established to send missionaries overseas, called the London Missionary Society. This was a tumultuous period in both colonial and naval history, and the LMS really struggled, at first, to even land missionaries in the target settings as a result. It was an age of pirates and revolutions (e.g. in France and America) when travel was fraught with dangers and ambiguities. In fact, most missionaries on their way to "the field" did not really count on returning to Europe (while many LMS missionaries were British, other nationalities were also recruited such as German and Dutch). There was no e-mail, no Facebook and no Skype, as there is now - 200 years later. One intrepid missionary in South India - a German named Ringeltaube - wrote regular letters to his sister from Nagercoil on the south tip of the Asian sub-continent. But not one of her replies succeeded in reaching him for his first five years there!

These missionaries were pioneers. Christianity was largely unknown in the places they were deployed by the LMS. And often they had to confront social evils that were embedded in local culture and practice.

Attrition rates were high – some missionaries quit because of the inherent hardships, and others succumbed to tropical diseases or martyrdom. Perhaps one of the most difficult challenges they had to contend with was loneliness. Local people spoke languages that they didn't understand at first, but they had to learn - so that they could translate Scripture into the vernaculars. Learning a new language as an adult can *feel* very humiliating, exacerbating the feeling of alienation triggered by social, cultural and religious divides.

Loneliness and Alienation

Missionaries were and are caught between two worlds. When pioneer missionaries reached Tahiti (then called the Society Islands) in Polynesia, they found terrifying levels of *infanticide*. When others reached China, they found that *foot-binding* was a prevailing practice – to intentionally disadvantage girls. In India, they confronted the rite of *suttee* – that is, burning a dead man's widow alive.

It is a challenge to preach God's love for all people while confronting such practices. These are the equivalent of corruption, "state capture" and cronyism today. We face the same conundrum – how to expose these social evils without alienating the very same people that we are here to serve.

Some missionaries were better received than others. For example, those that the LMS sent to the South Seas were posted on different islands – Tahiti, Marquesas, and Tonga. On Tahiti, the new king Pomare provided them upon arrival with some protection. He later converted to Christianity and became a patron of that mission, ardently involved in literacy and Bible translation.

Whereas in Marqueses, the reception was one of indifference. And worse yet, on Tonga, where it took two-and-a-half years for the next European ship to arrive, those who were dropped off initially had to endure unspeakable horrors. Three of the nine posted at Tonga were murdered; one renounced Christianity; and the remaining five had to hide in caves, living hand-to-mouth until that next European sailing vessel arrived. That mission was abandoned due to the hostile reception.

If you think in terms of a force-field analysis, the world that missionaries enter is only one force that they have to contend with. There is another side to it...

Closer to Home

Here in South Africa, the LMS deployed a Dutch missionary called Johannes van der Kemp. He and a Xhosa translator named Bruntjie set out from the Cape Colony for its eastern frontier, only to find themselves in the midst of fighting between the boers and the Xhosa chieftan Gaika. The missionary went boldly to Gaika's kraal to present his credentials and state his true intentions – and he was not unwelcome. So an initial mission house was built.

But before long, Gaika asked him to close it down because of continued fighting with the boers, so he relocated it. As the fighting spread, he had to close that second mission as well. So he took a third run at it, in the town of Graaff-Reinet, building a boarding school for the slaves working in and around the town.

When he began native prayer meetings in town, he started to receive death threats from the boers. One of the two new missionaries who had joined him there resigned because of this rising hostility. At one point, not less than 300 boer wagons assembled at Zwargershoek, to the extent that the nearest settlers fled from their farms. They expected an altercation between Dutch settlers and missionaries! This was only avoided by the intervention of British forces.

Not long after, boers rode into town and burned down the Khoi school. The missionary was chased by four "hired guns" who had been paid to take him out.

This settler resistance was and is the other side of the force-field that missionaries must contend with. William Carey reported that the British East India Company was adamantly opposed to the deployment of Christian missionaries. For it had immediately recognized the logic that a message of liberation and empowerment would have on its work force. In fact, Carey had to launch his mission in a Danish enclave on the coast of India.

In British Guyana, a thriving sugar exporting colony, the governor would not allow the LMS missionary to build a chapel for slaves in the colony's capital Georgetown. This matter was raised by William Wilberforce in the British parliament, which declared it illegal.

Nevertheless, on-the-ground realities were such that the governor would not give way during the remaining six months of his tenure. To diffuse the situation, the mission was moved to a province where the British government had allocated a crown estate as a mission station for freed slaves.

On another occasion in Guyana, a pregnant slave woman on a neighbouring estate was beaten so badly that she lost her baby. Again, a missionary travelled all the way to Britain, where he succeeded in gaining a conviction with a 3-month jail sentence for the perpetrator.

A similar perspective was articulated by a sea-captain (Riggs) who explained to a delegation of mission evaluators on his ship the *General Gates* (while moored off of Huahine in the Society Islands) - why sailors hate missionaries:

"Many seamen who touch at these islands expecting to revel, as of old, in all manner of impurity, are ready, in their rage and disappointment, to propagate the most atrocious slanders against these idolaters and their Christian instructors, through whose influence they are most wholly prevented from luring females on board their vessels."

"A Captain P., of the ship W., was so horribly provoked, when he was off here, that he threatened to fire a broadside, at his departure, on the innocent inhabitants, because they were more virtuous than himself, impudently telling them, that if any of them were killed, the Missionaries must bear the blame."

Suffice it to say that not all stakeholders, not even from the "sending countries" are delighted when the seed planted takes root, and grows tall, bearing much fruit. By the way, it was not long before native missionaries from Tahiti and Huahine set out themselves to spread the good news, literacy and to confront the practice of infanticide on other islands around Polynesia.

Inter-racial Marriage

Trevor Noah says that he was "Born a Crime"... no one knows better than him!

Indeed the practice of a foreign missionary marrying a native woman was frowned upon, not just by Grand Apartheid - where it was formally legislated against - but even by "best practice". There were exceptions that proved the rule – one of them being Johannes van der Kemp, who married the daughter of a widow of a Madagascan slave. The whole family was redeemed from slavery by van der Kemp. W.T. Ringeltaube met this family in the Cape on his passage out to India. Speaking of the bride's mother, he recorded: "There is no affection, no pretense; every word sounds as pure as if the spirit of the Lord were speaking through her." There is no substitute for simplicity and honesty. The inter-generational aspect of van der Kemp's marriage to the daughter was not always easy - for either of them.

The prevailing LMS practice was to recruit and send women missionaries to join the men *as their spouses*. Upon arrival in "the field", the more senior missionary got the first pick, and so forth, in descending order of seniority.

Tiyo Soga

With a little help from Willem Saayman's book <u>Christian Mission in South Africa</u>, I captured and re-jigged the following sketch of the first black ordained minister in South Africa... anchored in an inter-racial marriage.

Tiyo Soga was born in 1829. That was 186 years after Krotoa's birth; and 82 years after Johannes van der Kemp's birth.

By this time, missions were sprinkled all over the world including Africa and literacy, translation and schooling were their archetypical functions. So Tiyo Soga went to a mission school at primary level, then to Lovedale for high school. At this point, Lovedale was multiracial – but not co-ed!

During the war of 1846 he fled with the Scottish (Presbyterian) missionaries and was then taken to Scotland by a teacher at Lovedale, Mr Govan. (I am guessing that this teacher might have been Govan Mbeki's namesake?)

In 1848, while in Scotland, he was baptized and then returned to South Africa later the same year. He became a teacher in the Eastern

Cape. But he had to flee again with the missionaries during the 1850 war. In 1851 he travelled again to Glasgow in Scotland to study for the ministry. In 1856 he was ordained in the Presbyterian Church. In 1857 he married a Scottish women named Janet Burnside. Together they returned to serve as a missionary couple – first at Mgwali for 11 years, then at Tutura for 3 more years until his untimely death.

Willem Saayman uses a very good word to describe the love/hate relationship between colonialism and missions – "entanglement". While missions spread out largely in the slipstream of colonial expansion, the truth is that they were often at odds with business and government interests. Perhaps the best-known instance of this is the Abolitionist movement, which sought to bring an end to the Slave Trade. Obviously business interests opposed this on the whole, as did many government leaders. But key Christians like British MP William Wilberforce led the campaign to outlaw it. Missionaries around the world served as "observers" who collected and shared intelligence with the campaign, to bring it to an end. Without whistle-blowers, it might not have succeeded.

Just as it is unfair to say that native people were coerced into conversion, it is also unfair to generalize that missions endorsed colonialism.

One event stands out in Tiyo Soga's ministry – where he took a stand against the boys in his school taking the rites of initiation and circumcision. He saw this as "back-sliding" into traditional religion, which put him at odds with the parents of the learners enrolled in the mission school. This incident highlights the difficult position that he was in, as a black missionary.

Willem Saayman traces the roots of both African nationalism and Black Consciousness back to the life and work of Tiyo Soga.

Ironically perhaps, he chose to send is own coloured children off to school in Scotland, but on their departure he told them: *"take your place in the world as colored, not as white men, as Kaffirs not as English-*

men... For your own sakes never appear ashamed that your father was a Kaffir, and that you inherit some African blood"

Tiyo Soga was the only minister of the time who preached in congregations of all the protestant denominations of that period. So he not only planted seeds of African unity but of church unity as well.

Willem Saayman summarizes Tiyo Soga's influence as follows: *"It can be argued, then, that Soga left a legacy which is important today in the development of Black Consciousness and even pan-Africanism. This dimension of Soga's contribution flowed from his concern about the quality of life of his people in the oppressive colonial context. Because of this basic concern for people, Soga served as a symbol of unity already in his lifetime. As a loyal Presbyterian minister until his death, Soga can be seen as the role model of generations of African church people to come after him, people who were (and are) both consciously Christian and consciously African."*

Ambivalence

This word is used by Saayman to describe Tiyo Soga's way of living with the "entanglement" of colonialism and missions.

It is a word that could well be used to describe Krotoa's attitudes as well. She tried not to take sides, so to speak – she could see that engagement could be mutually beneficial to both sides.

Frankly I find it very hard to be ambivalent in my public engagement. When I see a Cabal appointing ministers and plundering parastatals in the context of a constitutional democracy, I get fired up. That is possibly my weak underbelly as a missionary change agent. I empathize with Lord Peter Hain in Britain who was an anti-apartheid campaigner before he entered the House of Lords. Now he is using his political influence to insist that the banks in the UK that have been used to launder money drained out of South Africa's economy by State Capture be exposed and that the funds be repatriated to South Africa. Amen!

Relevance

By the same token, I have become aware that there is still a popular narrative that the West wants "regime change" in South Africa, and that missionaries like me could be subversives. (As if citizens in a constitutional democracy aren't perfectly capable – *of their own volition* – to vote out one party, and to vote another one in!)

Opposition comes from both sides. The attitudes of whites towards Tiyo Soga were often openly racist and if there ever was a missionary caught between two worlds, it was Janet Burnside Soga!

Yet when her husband died, she did not race back to Scotland. She went to live with *his* mother for a period, at her village, so that all their children could become proficient in Xhosa before returning to Scotland. Then they returned to Scotland to complete their education. Only one of those children remained there for good. The others all returned to South Africa – including a doctor, a veterinarian, a magistrate, a teacher and a pastor. They worked in different settings including mission stations.

Of the four boys among those siblings, three paid their mother the high complement of also marrying Scottish women, and the other married a black South African.

If the proof of the pudding is in the eating, then there is no doubt that Tiyo Soga's inter-racial marriage served as an anchor for his "ambivalence" – which steered towards church unity, Pan-Africanism and Black Consciousness.

Asenath Hatch Nicholson

The *Oxford Biography Index* calls her a "social observer and philanthropist". Asenath Hatch Nicholson wrote the Annals of the Famine in Ireland which was published in 1851.

She had previously published Welcome to the Stranger in 1847, a valuable record of Ireland on the eve of the Famine. That is the account of her "first missionary journey" to Ireland in 1844 and 1845 which began when she left New York to "personally investigate the condition of the Irish poor" (her own words). This is an important "baseline study" because the purpose of that first visit was to distribute Bibles and read Scripture to the illiterate – not food aid. The background to this ministry is that she had been working with Irish immigrants in Brooklyn and felt a calling to go there as a missionary. In her days in New York she had been involved in both the Abolition and the Temperance movements. A broken marriage may have triggered her decision to "move on"?

In those days, being a Protestant "Bible reader" in a predominantly Catholic setting was regarded as proselytizing. She would distribute copies of the Bible to those who could read, and read the Bible to those who could not. Worse yet, Protestants were not generally supportive of her democratic ideals, including her being a 100% vegetarian. She was seen as something of a maverick – an American missionary to the Irish peasantry. She complained that people stared at her! After her first missionary journey to Ireland she left for Scotland in 1845. The emergence of the potato famine only started later that year.

She seemed to be the right person in the right place at the right time. She had now extensively traveled throughout Ireland and was busy generating a manuscript for her first book. Meanwhile her on-going correspondence had established a rapport with mission agencies and the Christian press. These contacts allowed her to appeal for relief aid as she started her second missionary journey to Ireland by setting up a soup kitchen in Dublin in late 1847. Soon some money and gifts-in-kind began to arrive in response to her personal appeals. As so often happens, church and non-state actors arrived at the scene of a disaster first and did what they could, followed in due course by government aid on a grander scale.

Church aid arrived on the same ships out of New York that brought hers, for the Central Relief Committee of the Society of Friends, but Nicholson preferred to operate individually.

She herself walked through Dublin every morning distributing slices of bread - not Bibles this time. Unlike the Quakers, she did not charge even a symbolic price, as she was targeting the poorest of the poor. She figured that £10 divided among 100 beneficiaries helped no one, so she tried to make a regular difference a target group.

By 1847 the government's Soup Kitchen Act (i.e. Temporary Relief Act) had kicked in, and she had finished her first manuscript. While it was being published, she followed the Quaker's lead of closing its Soup Kitchen in deference to government's aid scheme, and she began to visit the "interior" of Ireland again. It is from this period in Dublin and the famine- stricken West that her second book was drafted - Annals of the Famine in Ireland. It also came to be published – four years after her first book, in 1851. Her combined correspondence and publishing were a platform from which she pleaded the case (in today's jargonese) for Development being a higher good than Relief, and for "Trade not Aid". She argued this case with other philanthropists like English Quaker William Bennett. Her appeals were not only to friends and the public, but to government, which she also rebuked for corruption and its insensitivity. She regarded volunteer relief workers, coast guardsmen and missionaries as being much more sensitive and effective than bureaucratic government aid workers.

She herself lived frugally on bread and cocoa, and lamented loudly the diversion of grain to distilleries.

One important feature of her Annals is a record of how poor people helped one another. In fact, her Annals is really the third part of Lights and Shades of Ireland which she published at the end of her second missionary journey in London, in 1850. By then she thought the famine was over, but it recurred until 1852.

This week, St Patrick's Day was celebrated including the famous parade in New York. America has a huge Irish contingent which has made its mark. Many of these are descendants of people who left Ireland fleeing the famine.

But one maverick New Yorker left for Ireland on a personal mission of love which turned into a mission of mercy. Her work combines elements that are all dear to C4L – Bibles, literacy, disaster management, public engagement, fundraising, and writing books. These are all part of what we do or have done at C4L and we do it in the same spirit of "taking it personally" (i.e. small is beautiful) and yet working with other actors, while rebuking government at times, especially for corruption and insensitivity.

On a personal note, my own forefathers still lived in the West of Ireland at the time of Nicholson's two missionary journeys. *Maybe she visited them?* Only later in the 19th century did my great-grandfather O'Dowda emigrate to Canada. Thus the "thank you" in the title - to this role-model maverick missionary, Asenath Hatch Nicholson.

Americans have a special place in their heart for the Irish, and Ireland reciprocates. The feeling is mutual. She is one reason why.

Mission work has changed a lot over the centuries. But as the French say, *as everything changes, everything remains the same.*

Déjà vu from the Life of Abraham Lincoln

In his whole life, he spent less than a year in a classroom. He grew up on the frontier, moving from one rural setting to another as his father tried to find better land to farm. The law obliged him to work for his father until he was 21 – even though his Dad was abusive. He left home the day he turned 21 and years later refused to attend his own father's funeral. It was a strong statement. Some people interpret his unusual empathy with African slaves as deriving from his father's abuse and exploitation of him.

Abraham Lincoln taught himself how to read and write and he borrowed books whenever he could. After he left home, he wandered. He urbanized, he worked in different jobs. He kept studying and after three years he obtained his license to practice law. He was ambitious and determined to overcome the disadvantages he had grown up with. He joined a law firm and started a family, in Springfield, the state capital of Illinois.

I have to admit that this narrative resonates a bit with the upbringing of Nelson Mandela. The difference being that Abraham Lincoln, arguably America's greatest president, was not born into a royal family with any privileges at tribal level. Lincoln was the quintessential self-made man.

During a war with a local Indian tribe, he enlisted in the militia. His troop of men chose him to be their leader, an honour which he later said meant more to him than any other.

Suddenly he has a taste of leadership and those militia skirmishes would be his only military exposure prior to taking on the mantle of Commander in Chief at the outset of the bloody American Civil War.

He dabbled in local politics, gaining some experience in debate and public speaking. His first great policy challenge was to debate that Democracy was incompatible with Slavery. This was because some of the new territories to the west of Illinois were debating whether to legalize Slavery or not. He served two terms in the provincial legislature and one term in Washington, as a legislator, for the Whig party.

Then he ran for the Illinois seat in the Senate, but lost. It looked like the end of his political career; like he would have to be content with his law career.

But two years later, he managed to win the nomination to run for president under the newly formed Republican party. He won on the third round, as a compromise candidate, in Chicago.

He was physically awkward, ugly and so rural that he was considered too informal. Even after he moved into the White House, he would receive people at times in his bare feet. But he was so affable and honest that ordinary people could relate to him.

His first presidential race was against three other candidates. Fortunately for him, they split the vote, to the extent that he won - even though he had only garnered 39 percent of the votes. This election was virtually a referendum on the expansion of Slavery into the new states in the West. His victory stopped that. But it riled up the southern states, whose economy was based on Slavery.

In 2019 in South Africa, we can expect the elections to basically be a kind of referendum on another question - land expropriation without compensation. The debate is raging about that policy issue now, just as the expansion of Slavery issue was a raging debate in the years before Lincoln was elected.

His analysis was that Democracy was unfairly contrived because representation in Washington was disproportionate. This is because slaves were counted at three-fifths of a person (60 percent human) which gave the southern states an edge in the vote-counts, that in turn perpetuated the status quo. As a lawyer and a politician, Lincoln took exception to this, much like the citizens of South Africa objected to the structural injustices of colonialism and apartheid, and to contrivances like a tricameral Parliament.

In those days it was a two-week train trip to travel from Illinois to Washington. While making his way to Washington, for his inauguration, Lincoln learned that one state had seceded from the Union. Others followed, and soon they joined in a Confederacy. To Lincoln, this was illegal and treacherous, as the Union had even preceded the Constitution.

South Africa needs to think through the "repercussions" of what will happen if land is expropriated without compensation, particularly if the Constitution is changed to streamline that. For there could be knock-on effects - on the banks, on foreign investment, on race relations, and so forth. At the root of this is the notion of private property, which to some citizens is sacrosanct. That is not my personal belief, for I believe that the land belongs to God. I therefore endorse proactive Land Reform, but always in the context of the Rule of Law, and in a way that bonds different races together - not one that shakes Non-racialism.

There are such strategies, though some regard these as too "moderate" and not "radical" enough.

One can see an evolution in Lincoln's thinking over time. The American Civil War began as an attempt to keep the Union intact, preventing any states from seceding – an act of treason. In fact, Slavery was still legal in four states of the Union which Lincoln could not dare to lose. But in the early years of the war, it went badly for the North. They started with superior troop numbers, but these were depleted by very heavy casualties. Then Lincoln took a step that was not even considered at the beginning of the Civil War. He started to enlist black troops. He racially-integrated the army.

This inspired him to return to his arguments against the expansion of Slavery into new states in the West. That had not make him an "Abolitionist" back then, when he had been prepared just to contain it in the states where it already existed. But when he composed the Emancipation Declaration in the middle of the Civil War, it was a game-changer. He moved the goalposts from keeping the Union intact, to liberating slaves. This position was controversial even in the North. In fact, it was a white supremacist in the North who assassinated Lincoln, soon after the war was won.

Meanwhile, Lincoln managed to pass the Thirteenth Amendment, freeing the slaves. He managed to win the war after four years of bloodshed on a scale never seen before. And he managed to win a second presidential election. Only to be assassinated soon thereafter.

Looking back, Lincoln was elected with very little education and almost no experience in the executive branch of government. Nor did he have any military experience to speak of. Yet he led the Union to victory on the battlefield, thereby keeping the Union intact. The republican experiment in America got a new lease on life. On the way, he freed the slaves, a moral and social victory on top of his military and political successes. And he was only 56 years old when he was assassinated by an extremist.

South Africa seems to want to elect leaders who are already in their sixties or seventies, even though life expectancy here is only 50 years for men. So many competent young cadres are being overlooked. It seems almost silly for Zimbabwe to elect a 75-year-old to start a new era.

Lincoln was thrifty and honest. These are not virtues that come to mind in South Africa, where leaders have two distinct vices – waste and corruption. Waste is not illegal, it is just immoral in a country with so much poverty. Corruption is illegal, and is a cancer that weakens the country's economy and morale.

Above all, if Land Reform is an imperative – and I believe that it is – why can't it evolve slowly like Lincoln's thinking? Why do we suddenly need to amend the Constitution?

Certainly the Abolition movement was active, but Lincoln himself was no radical. He was a lawyer, a politician and ultimately a statesman. This takes patience and moves with glacial slowness at times. Slowly but surely. Sequentially. Cautiously.

"When you want to go fast, go alone. When you want to go far, go together."

9. PIONEERS

The dwindling influence of Henry George

By 1955, when the Freedom Charter was drafted in South Africa, at the Congress of the People, two foreign names had come to capture political and economic discourse – Adam Smith of the UK and Karl Marx of Germany. Call them right wing and left wing respectively.

By then, comparatively few people remembered the name of an American whose writings had arguably greater influence than either of these two economic prophets – Henry George. Smith wrote <u>The Wealth of Nations</u> first, in 1776. Then Marx wrote <u>Das Kapital</u> in 1867. George wrote <u>Progress and Poverty</u> in 1879, and <u>Protection and Free Trade</u> in 1886.

Henry George was concerned about poverty, inequality and unemployment. Sound familiar? He wrote about issues like natural monopolies, contrived privileges, economic rent, and the socialization of land and natural resources. His thoughts certainly line up with the excerpts of the Freedom Charter cited above. George's message attracts support widely across the political spectrum, including labour union activists, socialists, anarchists, libertarians, reformers, conservatives, and wealthy investors. As a result, George is still claimed as a primary intellectual influence by both classical liberals and socialists. Here are some of the policies that he advocated:

- Free trade as opposed to protectionism
- Free market as opposed to a planned economy
- Secret ballot
- Debt jubilee
- A basic income or "citizen's dividend"
- LVT (land value tax) including tax on natural resources

He argued that while people should own the value that they produce themselves, economic value derived from <u>land</u> (and he applied the same to <u>natural resources</u>) should belong equally to all members of society. You do not have to confiscate the land from productive citizens to guarantee this mutual benefit. As in the Year of Jubilee, the land can be *re-divided amongst those who work it.*

Advocates of LVT argue that it would reduce economic inequality, increase economic efficiency, remove incentives to under-utilize urban land and reduce property speculation. The philosophical basis of George's thinking dates back to several early thinkers such as John Locke, Baruch Spinoza and Thomas Paine. However the concept of gaining public revenues mainly from land and natural resource privileges was widely popularized by Henry George in his book <u>Progress and Poverty</u>.

I should also mention that Henry George and Karl Marx, who lived at the same time, were antagonists. Marx saw the LVT platform as a step backwards from the transition to communism. On his part, Henry George predicted that if Marx's ideas were tried, the likely result would be a dictatorship.

Just listen to the list of those who sang the praises of Henry George!

- A 1906 survey of British parliamentarians revealed that the American author's writing was more popular than Walter Scott, John Stuart Mill and William Shakespeare
- By 1908, two years before his death, Tolstoy had become obsessed with George's LVT, regarding it as vital for the moral and economic regeneration not only of his homeland, but of the world
- Father Edward McGlynn, one of the most prominent and controversial Catholic priests of the time, was quoted as saying, "That book is the work of a sage, of a seer, of a philosopher, of a poet. It is not merely political

philosophy. It is a poem; it is a prophecy; it is a prayer."

- In 1933, John Dewey estimated that Progress and Poverty "had a wider distribution than almost all other books on political economy put together."
- Alfred Russel Wallace hailed Progress and Poverty as "undoubtedly the most remarkable and important book of the present century," placing it even above Charles Darwin's On the Origin of Species. Only one book outsold it during the decade after its release – the Bible.
- Albert Einstien wrote this about his impression of Progress and Poverty: "Men like Henry George are rare unfortunately. One cannot imagine a more beautiful combination of intellectual keenness, artistic form and fervent love of justice. Every line is written as if for our generation. The spreading of these works is a really deserving cause, for our generation especially has many and important things to learn from Henry George."
- Franklin D Roosevelt praised George as "one of the really great thinkers produced by our country" and bemoaned the fact that George's writings were not better known and understood
- Among many famous people who asserted that it was impossible to refute George on the land question were Winston Churchill and Bertrand Russell
- The anti-war activist Rev John Haynes Holmes echoed that sentiment by commenting that George was "one of the half-dozen great Americans of the nineteenth century, and one of the outstanding social reformers of all time."

Commentators disagreed on whether Henry George's funeral was the largest ever in New York history, or just the largest since the death of Abraham Lincoln. *The New York Times* reported, "Not even Lincoln had a more glorious death."

So when there are centrist solutions like LVT to the vexing issue of Land Reform, why, I wonder, are we rushing into EWC?

It seems to me that the ANC has not done its homework. I bet that most Cabinet members have never even heard the name Henry George? Yet his ideas may have more relevance to South Africa's rural land reform that the solutions offered by Marxism. We do not need extremism at either end of the political spectrum, both of which challenge social cohesion. We need tolerance and a "progressive" approach. We need South Africans to find one another, not contrived, top-down government intervention.

Davos 2020 identified "polarization" as one of the three main problems in today's world. During the 20th century, largely due to the impetus of Henry George, 90 percent of voters converged on the Centre-Right or Centre-Left. This issue of The Weighbridge treats these both as "centrist".

In the 21st century, only 40 percent of voters are in this zone – many have switched to Alt-Right or Far Left. Is this progress? It is pulling democracy apart. Instead of integrating views in a way that promotes social cohesion, this is having a dis-integrating effect on societies. United we stand, divided we fall.

The Betta Einders

From Bitter-einders to Hens-oppers - to Betta-einders

After the second Anglo-Boer War in South Africa, the British offered amnesty to the diehard guerrilla commandos who did not want to capitulate. A similar phenomenon happened after World War II in the Pacific theatre, where Japanese soldiers had been dropped on remote islands to defend them during the conflict. Perhaps even unaware that the war was over, they remained dangerous hold-outs long after peace broke out.

In Afrikaans, these commandos were called the "bitter-einders" and it was the invention of concentration camps that had especially embittered them. One can understand their depth of emotions. The other school of thought was to surrender or to accept the post-war amnesty offered by the British. Those who did so were called the "hens-oppers" – because the put their hands up. This was not a complimentary term, to put it mildly.

Before long, the real-politic focus shifted from English-versus-Boers to blacks-versus-whites. But in several ways that I can think of, the two labels remain relevant even today. In the 2019 elections, some of the "centrist" vote shifted. The "broad church" ANC lost some ground (and seats in Parliament) to the Leftist EFF. And the "near right" DA lost some ground (and seats) to the Alt Right Freedom Front Plus. For this reason, I generally refer to both the EFF and the FF+ as "extremist" parties. Neither wants to put their hands up.

Malema vocalizes a lot of the "bitter-einder" attitude against whites. One can well understand his/their bitterness, given the history of exploitation and oppression of blacks by whites. But not all blacks – among them Nelson Mandela – were "bitter-einders". Madiba did not have to surrender, so he was not a "hens-opper". He emerged magnanimous. And yet in spite of the obvious examples of Zimbabwe, Venezuela and the former "East Bloc" of Europe, the socialist rhetoric continues unabated from the far-Left.

I do not dispute the right of the white tribe of Africa to self-determination. But many of the 30 000 boers (i.e. farmers) who possess about 70 percent of the arable land in South Africa are diehards. They are not going to be easy to move, and that intransigence could be why the ANC has taken its cue from the EFF and decided to go forward with EWC (expropriation without compensation). To my way of thinking, taking such measures is risky, and could provoke a back-lash from the Alt Right.

The risk that I see is Partition, as happened not that long ago in India and Pakistan. Otherwise known as the "two-state solution". And this is not such a wild card. Orania is already on the map, and the Zulus are not sold on socialist solutions to Land Reform. In Ethiopia, Sidama is on the rise, seeking more regional autonomy.

God forbid that it should start an insurgency, like Eritrea once did, to break away. Now in Europe we see cases like Catalonia and Scotland where authentic ethnic groups want their independence. I worry that pushing the Afrikaner too hard on this issue could lead to a split.

So I am advocating a CENTRIST SOLUTION to Land Reform. I admit that this has been inspired by the "Year of Jubilee" which the Bible calls for – on a once-in-a-lifetime basis. But I will stop the Bible-thumping and concisely outline five variations on that theme. Any or all of them could work as CENTRIST SOLUTIONS to Land Reform.

AA – This stands for <u>Accept Amnesty</u> but don't dismiss it as putting your hands up in surrender. In our generation, it is inspired by *The Giving Pledge* that Bill Gates and Warren Buffet have been promoting for a decade. These guys are capitalists, not communists. They encourage billionaires to give away 50 percent of their wealth. Farmers may protest that they are not billionaires. My reply is that to a poor and unemployed youth, living in a township, you might as well be. One way to do this would be to cash-out your farm. Keep the proceeds from the sale of all your "movables" – machinery, stock, investments, etc... BUT DONATE YOUR LAND. (My assumption is that about half of your nett worth is tied up in your land.)

Do not give your land over to government. Only transfer the title of your land IN ESGROW into the name of a Jubilee Land Bank. My suggestion is that every District should have such a land bank, basically a Trust that is governed by Public-Private Partnership. These land banks must hold land donated for at least seven years, until the productivity and commitment of emerging black farmers can be verified. Only then can authentic food-producing new owners receive land title - for free. If their agri-business efforts fail, the farm remains in esgrow with the Land Bank until it is under productive new management.

BB – This stands for <u>Body Building</u>. In other words, the white farmer should decentralize and create an enabling, entrepreneurial environment for emerging black farmers. Find ways for them to operate "concessions". Some might run a repair shop for tractors and machinery? Others might run a nursery to prepare seedlings? Others might run the farm canteen or tuck shop? In other words, replace the "homogenized" structure with a "conglomerate" structure. One variation of this is called "share-cropping". But that model held back those working the land from owning it. In this BB model, provision should be built in for some kind of ownership.

C – By this I refer to a <u>Circle</u> of friends. For example, ten boers could form a Circle and draw lots. One of the ten by this lottery mechanism must give over his or her land to the Jubilee Land Bank (as outlined above). The others form a solidarity group which commits to support the "loser" of the lottery. They might set up a processing plant, for example, which s/he manages. Either a coop or a company – that guarantees employment for the farmer who lost his land. All the other nine farmers stand behind it. In doing so, they are standing behind Jubilee.

D – This stands for <u>Downsize</u>. It's as simple as streamlining your own operation to make room for some "HDI" farmers. They are also South African citizens. One goal of the NDP is to reduce the Gini coefficient. That is the principle of Jubilee in a different language. Make room.

EEE – By this I mean <u>Emigrate and Export Expertise</u>. After the Anglo-Boer War, some of the "bitter-einders" left for Patagonia. There was another wave of emigration after 1994. The truth is that the white population has shrunk since 1994 – although not all were going to farm in their new settings. But there are countries that are in desperate need of competent, experienced farmers. This is a "critical skill shortage" – for example in Australia. My advice would be for the younger generation of the family farm to go first, and get settled. Then for the older boer to divest all the "movables" and take that money with them for their retirement – but donate their land to the Jubilee Land Bank.

These are just sketchy examples of CENTRIST SOLUTIONS. As President Ramaphosa recently said, Land Reform is an imperative, and we need to "find one another" on this issue. Extremism and polarization are dangerous. The land, after all, belongs to God. Not to the State nor to any human. You might have made barns, silos or irrigation system, but God made the land and the water. "The cattle on a thousand hills belong to Him." Blacks and whites largely agree on this baseline of belief.

In the UK they speak of "leavers" and "remainers". I am pleased to hear that a group of young Afrikaners have actually adopted the name "betta-einders" - in an ironic way. They are saying, We are going nowhere, South Africa is our home, so we will tough it out through thick and thin. They do not say this as "hard liners" of the Alt Right. They are Centrists and Christians, and they want constitutional democracy to work. God bless these remainers. They are not traitors like those who General Koos de la Rey respected even while he fought the British. Those "veraillers" simply saw the futility of enlisting in an unwinnable war. Could history be repeating itself?

Marie Curie - Selflessness

What is it like for a person to be "selfless"?

Marya Sklodowska was born in Poland in 1867. Like Nelson Mandela, she was born in one century, and died in the next - in a new and different era. That change in their respective settings and centuries could be attributed largely to the influence each of them exerted in their sphere.

Like Mandela, Marya came from a disadvantaged background. She too was a single orphan, she lost her mother as a child, whereas Mandela lost his father. But compared to Mandela - who enjoyed the limelight - Marya cherished privacy. Later in life, when she won her second Nobel prize, her husband stated that the media attention that this attracted was the worst thing that had ever happened to them!

Mandela's life took a turn when he moved to the big city of Johannesburg. In Marya's case, the sea change came when she got to Paris. Both of them spent their first few years completing their studies and struggling to get established in their respective professions – he as a lawyer and she as a scientist. In their cities, they each got married – Nelson to Evelyn and Marya to Pierre Curie. So she became better known by her francophone name Marie and her married name Curie. She has come to be known, in fact, as Madame Curie. Yet I have never known of a person who was more selfless:

- After finishing high school she put her own education on hold and worked to put her older sister through college. After graduating from medical school, her sister reciprocated
- She practiced an austerity that verged on self-denial. She rented small rooms that were so sparsely furnished that she didn't even hang pictures on the wall!
- With a wedding gift she received, she bought two bicycles that she and her groom used for the honeymoon – pedaling through the countryside of France
- She worked in abysmal conditions, far beyond the limits of normal working hours - all for the sake of her passion for scientific research
- She declined to patent any of her discoveries or inventions, leaving them instead to posterity for the advancement of science

- She shared much of her prize money with others in need, in part to establish two radium research institutes – in Paris and Warsaw
- She worked behind the front lines of battle in World War I training 150 X-ray technicians to use this new diagnostic tool that she had developed to locate bullets and shrapnel for removal from wounded soldiers
- She exposed herself to radioactivity levels that shortened her life. She died of leukemia induced by overexposure, before her time

She was the first women ever to be awarded a PhD in France. And the first woman ever to win a Nobel prize. And the first person ever to win Nobel prizes in two different sciences – Physics (1903) and Chemistry (1911).

In this respect, the parallel to Nelson Mandela refers. At Marie Curie's time in France, it was unthinkable for a woman to even be nominated for a Nobel laureate. In fact, she wasn't – her husband and another scientist (Henri Becquerel) were. But in more liberal Sweden, the Nobel committee awarded her the prize nevertheless, realizing that she was being discriminated against. Who could have dreamed that after 3 decades of incarceration.

Mandela would become President? Both scenarios were breathtaking – and rooted in selflessness. Justice and "the beauty of science" were paramount to them.

One irony is that Alfred Nobel himself had made his personal fortune from discovering and patenting dynamite. Upon his death, he bequeathed that fortune to fund the Nobel prizes. Either one of Marie Curie's discoveries could have been patented far beyond the value of dynamite – Xray and radioactivity. (It was she, in fact, who coined that word "radioactivity" to describe what she had discovered.) Yet she declined to register patents for the sake of "pure science" for its own sake. Excellence is its own reward.

"True grit" is part of selflessness as well. Mandela toughed it out in prison for 27 years for the cause he championed. He did hard labour in the lime quarry on Robben Island. Like Marie Curie, his own health was affected by his exposure – in his case, to the fine dust, that damaged his tear ducts.

As for Marie, it is almost inconceivable just how much physical work she did! Processing uranium ore (pitchblende) to refine *polonium* and later *radium* is painstaking, time- consuming hard labour. In this, she was her own prisoner. The final product turned out to be one-millionth the volume that you start with (compared to one litre of maple syrup which is boiled down from 30 litres of tree sap!) Imagine – one million to one... processed by one person working by herself for about 4 years. It was back breaking work. Marie's resolve is epitomized in this quote... she said: "One never notices what has been done; one can only see what remains to be done."

She was also very loyal – for example, naming Polonium after her beloved homeland.

Albert Einstein said: "Marie Curie is, of all celebrated beings, the only one whom fame has not corrupted." In this, her selflessness is also similar to Mandela's – whose movement became horribly corrupt after his voluntary retirement.

Which makes me wonder...

Have we lost an appreciation for virtues like selflessness, zealous resolve, prudence, and tenacious loyalty?

Have these been corrupted into attitudes like self-preservation, cynicism, a preoccupation with credentials and track records, and fashion crazes?

At the root of Corruption are bad attitudes. Let us adopt role-models that serve as mirrors.

We are marching to Pretoria!

Last year, when I marched with Save South Africa in Pretoria, I was humming this tune. But I kept it to myself!

We don't hear much of this old martial song any more. For it is less that politically correct, with roots in colonialism that were then adapted to a song about the Boer War. Probably either side in that conflict could claim it, as the British won the war... but the Boers won the peace.

Perhaps the most memorable march in Pretoria was in August 1956 – *the Women's March* – to protest the pass-laws for black women under Grand Apartheid. The cracks in both racial and gender discrimination were starting to show.

In March 1960 there was an infamous march in Sharpeville. By the time it was over, 500 citizens had perished. It was also about pass-books.

In June 2018, on Youth Day, we remember them marching in Soweto, in 1976. The photo- journalist who captured that iconic scene has just been laid to rest. RIP Sam Nzime.

The civil rights movement in the USA was also organizing many famous marches there, at the time. The most memorable was a march on Washington in August 1963. Here is a paraphrase of a speech made on that day by the Reverend Martin Luther King Jr. If he was marching in 2018 it would probably be to Pretoria – for the cause of Youth.

We come to our nation's rulers to cash a check

When the architects of our republic wrote the magnificent words of the Constitution, they were signing a promissory note to which every South African was to fall heir

This note was a promise that all women and men Yes, young as well as old would be guaranteed paying work and sufficiency

It is obvious today that the nation has defaulted on this promissory note

insofar as so many of her citizens are unemployed

Instead of honoring this sacred obligation,
South Africa has given its youth a bad check,
a check that has come back marked "insufficient funds."
But we refuse to believe that the bank of justice is bankrupt.
We refuse to believe that there are insufficient funds in the great
vaults of resources and opportunity in this nation.
And so we've come to cash this check,
a check that will give us upon demand the riches of freedom and
security of justice.
We have also come to this hallowed indaba to remind South Africa of
the fierce urgency This is no time to engage in the luxury of fat-cat
salaries
or to take the tranquilizing drug of patronage
Now is the time to make real the promises of democracy.
Now is the time to rise from the dark and desolate valley of
corruption to the sunlit path of honesty and transparency
Now is the time to lift our nation from the quicksands of malpractice
to the solid rock of integrity
Now is the time to make justice a reality for all of God's children.

10. POLITICIANS

Tommy Douglas – Déjà vu all over again

A wave of populism has been rising behind a new party called the Economic Freedom Fighters. They are led by another "radical dissenter" called Julius Malema. There are some amazing parallels between him and Canada's Tommy Douglas, who formed the first social democratic government ever in North America - the CCF. That really stood for Co-operative Commonwealth Federation, because it promoted co-op models - from agriculture to banking. Thus its critics dubbed the CCF "Communize Canada through Fear". Douglas responded that it rather stood for "Children Come First".

His roots had been in the church – his career, which started as a Baptist minister, coincided with the beginning of the Great Depression. At that time, farming had not mechanized to the extent that it has since, so Saskatchewan was the third most populous province in Canada (900 000 people in 1930). It was populated by farmers from all around the world, who had converged on the Canadian prairies following the launch of Durham wheat in the 1890s - which could be grown at such northern latitudes.

As a man of the cloth during that era, he was no stranger to humanitarian assistance. He spent a lot of his time working with unemployed youth in particular. As a pastor he wanted to fight for social justice as well, but his church elders gave him an ultimatum - to choose between running for public office and the ministry. So he decided to run in his Weyburn riding for a new party called the CCF - in national elections. He was elected by his riding and cut his teeth in politics as an MP representing his constituency in the national capital, Ottawa. In Canadian Parliament.

The parallels between Tommy Douglas/CCF and Julius Malema/EFF go on... Both entered politics as youth. In fact, Malema was the leader of the ANC Youth League and still has solid support from that core constituency – youth. However, like Douglas, his elders/bosses ran him out of the organization that he loved – so he decided to run for office on the merits of his own track record and convictions. This makes them both "radical dissenters".

The EFF party was launched, symbolically, in Marikana. There is another striking parallel (pun intended). For it was observing the joint hostility of mine owners and police against miners - during a strike at Estevan, Saskatchewan – that shook Douglas out of his complacency and comfort as a church leader, into the political arena. What happened at Marikana was a repeat performance, 80 years later.

When the CCF eventually decided to run a full slate of candidates in Saskatchewan's provincial elections, Douglas decided to resign as a national MP and lead the party in his province. He ran on a platform of "public ownership". This in not unlike the Economic Freedom Fighters, whose manifesto includes nationalizing some mines, and expropriating some farms.

Tommy Douglas' detractors tried to label him a Bolshevik, a Communist, and so forth. (One has to remember that the great excesses of Lenin had not yet come to light in the 1930s and Stalin had just come to power.) But he was not an ideologue - he was basically a kind, honest, forward-looking chap... a straight-ahead guy. He did not finish high school before entering an apprenticeship in the printing trade. But he completed his studies in order to enter seminary, where he merged the evangelical and social gospels. Decades after his death, a poll in Canada rated him the most influential Canadian – ever.

<u>Tony Benn</u>
We need more Radical Dissenters

By birth, Tony Benn was an aristocrat. By persuasion, he was a Leftist.

Such principled leaders are rare. Tony Benn was elected to the House of Commons at 25, but his parliamentary career seemed to come to an abrupt end in 1961 when his father died. As the new Viscount Stansgate, he was barred from the Commons so that he could take up membership in the unelected upper House of Lords. For three years he battled to change the law to allow hereditary peers to renounce their titles. Voters in his parliamentary district of Bristol West elected him once more, even though he couldn't take his seat in the Commons. In 1963, the bill passed, and the Times of London declared, "Lord Stansgate will be Mr. Benn today."

He is remembered as "champion of the powerless. The British PM said: *He was a magnificent writer, speaker, diarist and campaigner, with a strong record of public and political service.*"

Ed Miliband, Labour Party leader at the time of his death, said: "*Tony Benn spoke his mind and spoke up for his values. Whether you agreed with him or disagreed with him, everyone knew where he stood and what he stood for. For someone of such strong views, often at odds with his party, he won respect from across the political spectrum. This was because of his unshakable beliefs and his abiding determination that power and the powerful should be held to account.*"

Benn favoured abolition of the monarchy, British withdrawal from the European Union, and any strike that was going, hadn't changed. His image evolved from a demonized figure in the 70s and 80s to that often-treasured English archetype: *the radical dissenter*. Tony Benn renounced his aristocratic title rather than leave the House of Commons.

Incarnational Mission

"*He came into the world, and the world was made by Him, and the world knew him not.*" This is not just a story of alienation, it is role-modeling – how to be downwardly mobile. He left the security and privileges of being the only Son of the Father, and he pitched his tents among us. He was despised and rejected of men. He was a man of sorrows and acquainted with grief.

Tommy Douglas often recited the political fable first told by Clarence Gillis called <u>Mouseland</u>. It is a send-up of Capitalism, along the same lines of <u>Animal Farm</u> which sends up Communism. I have adapted it every so little to fit the South African setting.

But there is a lot of gospel truth in this parable. Now the question is, whether what has happened in Canada over the decades will happen in South Africa this year? To express disapproval of their favorite party, Canadian voters tend not to stop voting for them, but to split their votes – that is to vote for a different party in the province that they vote for federally. In South Africa, there are no provincial elections, just Municipal – and they are coming up in August 2016. To date, voters tend to communicate their discontent by burning down government infrastructure while ironically voting the ruling alliance back in! Has the time come that they will cast their Municipal vote in a different direction? That's what got the CCF elected in Saskatchewan, and it went on to win five consecutive provincial elections!

11. THE FOUR GOSPELS OF OUR TIME

There are many variations of this tale, but four exemplary church leaders come to mind from the past century:

1. Dietrich Bonhoeffer's stand against the Holocaust
2. Martin Luther King's stand against Segregation
3. John-Paul II's stand against Communism
4. Desmond Tutu's stand against Apartheid

Bonhoeffer

He was born into a well-to-do aristocratic family before World War I. As a teenager he decided to become a theologian, although his siblings were eminent scientists and lawyers - like so many of his relatives were. After completing his doctorate at age 21, he spent periods of time working in Spain, the USA and England, so he was able to see Fascism for what it truly was, when it emerged between the two World Wars. His ecumenical and global contacts provided a counter-balance to run-away German nationalism.

The dark side of Hitler promoting an Arian super-race was that he singled out a minority for genocide. These ideas were somewhat in line with social Darwinism the scientific trending of that era. But they did not align with historical Christian values and beliefs. This did not deter Hitler and his inner circle from planning to corrupt theology, systematically absorb the church, and then redeploy it. For example, in 1933 the new "Reich Church" was told to merge ALL church youth groups with the Hitler Youth movement. The state church was to become a cultural institution to support the Third Reich. The philosopher Nietzsche became its prophet (e.g. "Morality is the herd-instinct in the individual"). The contrast to Martin Luther's theology was shocking – instead of Grace, the Reich Church worshipped Power. Its bishop was a former Navy chaplain.

Bonhoeffer opposed this hijacking of the Protestant church and declared the Reich Church's theology to be heretical. First he started a Pastors Emergency League and later the underground Confessional Church. In due course, during World War II, this led him to get personally involved in a plot to assassinate Hitler - as the extent of Nazi Anti-Semitism with its death camps and extermination of the mentally ill became clearer. But for his role in this failed attempt at regime change, he was sentenced to death for treason.

All the same, he is truly revered by churches everywhere as a Protestant saint – for coming to the rescue of the Jews in the face of state-sanctioned genocide.

Martin Luther King

He was also a pastor, but not a Lutheran in spite of his middle name! He was a great orator - like Bonhoeffer. In the mid-1950s, he took up a political cause – the segregation of schools, buses and restaurants, and the practice of not allowing blacks to vote that prevailed in some southern states.

Like Bonhoeffer, he was well-known to the authorities. By the time Lyndon Johnson became President, King was on a roll. He visited the Oval office more than once. He took his mission to Selma, Alabama, to march to the state capital and demand to register black voters. The march across the bridge at Selma in 1965 turned into a Sharpeville scenario – 5 years after the incident in South Africa. Covered by the media - on national TV - this encounter galvanized support from other states and countries. Effectively, the federal government had to intervene and tell the state government to "correct" its ways.

Unlike the Jews in Germany, African-Americans were an underclass. German Jews were well-to-do and well-educated. Names like Freud and Einstein come to mind. But African Americans – even a century after the Civil War ended slavery – were still a marginalized minority. The Civil Rights Movement gradually changed all that. Of course there are still nasty attitudes that linger, but they are not prevalent. The election and re-election of President Obama was evidence of that.

Karol Wojtyla

He grew up in Communist Poland. It was part of the "East Bloc" namely eastern Europe which was controlled by the Soviet Union.

Poland had a proud history of being independent and of course resented its occupation by Russia. It was and is a devoutly Roman Catholic country, and had put forth great heroes like Marie Curie, who won two Nobel prizes - in two distinct disciplines. Wojtyla stayed true to his faith, his role-models, and decided to go to Seminary even though the church was experiencing persecution in all of eastern Europe and the Soviet Union.

Every "struggle" can put forward secular heroes as well as church leaders. In Germany one thinks of courageous citizens like Sophie Scholl. In America, musicians like Woodie Guthrie and Peter Seeger come to mind. In South Africa, a lawyer and activist called Nelson Mandela. In Poland, it was a plumber in the trade union Solidarity, called Lech Walesa.

When he climbed over a fence to come over and speak to the media, it was clear that the fear of oppression was waning. Holes were rusting through the iron curtain! That was in 1980. The Berlin Wall came down in 1989. Between these two dates there was Glasnost first, then Perestroika in Russia. Welesa went on to become President of Poland!

One factor may have sparked Solidarity's courage in 1980 – the election of a Polish Pope in 1978. This was a prophetic act, if there ever was one. The Curia's strategy in electing Karol Wojtyla to be Pope John Paul II may have been unspoken, but he did not miss his cue. John Paul II was a man on a mission, and that political objective came to pass – on his watch. The "Second World" all but disappeared, leaving only the First World and the Third World to trundle on under a single superpower. Except for its vestiges in Cuba and North Korea, Communism crashed.

Apartheid was able to hang on as long as it did because of its shared anti-Communist position. However, by the time Mandela was moved from Robben Island to Pollsmoor Prison in 1982 it was clear that even the Boers were hatching a contingency plan. Winds of change were blowing.

The question of Sanctions was vexing. In the 1980s, many including the UK's Maggie Thatcher argued that it would actually hurt blacks in South Africa more than it would help their cause, because of the negative impact it would have on the economy. Commonwealth leaders kept up the pressure on her and the UK to relent and impose economic sanctions.

Desmond Tutu

At the time, the South Africa Council of Churches had a general secretary who had started his career as a teacher. Then when Afrikaans was imposed as the medium of instruction in all schools, he changed his career path, and went to seminary. He became the first black (Anglican) bishop in South Africa. As general secretary of the SACC, he was invited to visit Denmark, and while there, he was interviewed on television. Although he was a pastor and a theologian, he signaled his support. Upon his arrival back in Johannesburg, he was visited by the secret police. They gave him 24 hours to publicly retract his statement, which had made the world news.

That night, as he agonized over what to do, his wife Leah said that she would rather see him happy on Robben Island, than miserable at home in Soweto! Women of influence include Bonhoeffer's mother and of course Coretta King, who never remarried after he husband was assassinated in 1968.

Tutu did not recant his view. But he was not arrested after all, because of the ecumenical and international support that he commanded. It was just more of the intimidation church leaders get from speaking truth to power.

These vignettes of four gospels – to the Jews, the African American, the Poles living under Russian domination, and the blacks of South Africa – are related for a reason...

How can a President say – at a church conference yet! – that the church should stay out of public life?!

Does he want our churches to become like the Reich Church? Heretical in its absolution of government crimes? There has been no genocide in South Africa, but there has been xenophobia, patronage, corruption and waste. And there was an African genocide – in Rwanda – during the years of Mandela's presidency.

No, the church has a mission. The gospel is told and re-told in different settings, situationally. South Africa is well evangelized and deeply religious. Among its greatest leaders are churchmen like John Dube and Albert Luthuli. *The light is shining in the darkness, and the darkness will never put it out.*

12. MINSTRELS

Pete Seeger

We lament the departure of this great artist and human being yesterday.

When Seeger wrote *If I had a hammer* in 1949, Bono was but a twinkle in his father's eye. But that song has become like our International anthem.

I wrote the tribute below in 2007 - to my own father on the occasion of his winning of the Order of Canada for humanitarian service. It was never before posted as a C4L Bulletin, so this is not a re-run. All I can say is this gives you some idea of the stature of Pete Seeger - the yardstick against which I measure greatness.

The Bible and the Almanac

In the 1940s, two musical groups were formed which would have a great influence on my life. One was called the Med's Gospel Team, in Canada, because the members were all studying medicine. One of the team members would later get married and become my father. The other was called the Almanac Singers, in the USA, which included Pete Seeger and Woodie Guthrie. Obviously the emphasis of these groups differed – one was evangelistic and the other was social/cultural. The better known group (by far) had chosen its name out of its belief that most farm homes had two books – a Bible and an almanac.

Maybe this explains why my two favorite forms of music are hymns and protest songs? I love to hear my father playing hymns on the piano, and I still agree with Pete Seeger's comment at the 1965 Newport Folk Festival – when he said he wished that he had an axe to cut the cord of Bob Dylan's microphone! This because Dylan had just been accompanied by the Paul Butterfield Blues Band, and no one could hear the message in his music.

As a young man, Pete Seeger embraced the conviction that songs are a way of binding people to a cause. John and Charles Wesley were the minister and the musician that launched Methodism. Seeger's father - a music academic - wrote that the necessary question to ask was not "Is it good music?" but "What is the music good for?"

Pete Seeger's influence is amazing. Dylan was not just Seeger's heir apparent, perhaps more of his legitimization. Johnny Cash was but a teen idol until he re-recorded his song *Folsom Prison Blues* in a new setting – not in a concert hall or recording studio, but live at Folsom Prison. Songs like *Man in Black,* that influenced me personally, put deeper meaning in the music and that placed Cash (the other JC in my life) in a whole new league. He in turn influenced others - like Bono, who in the Cash tradition usually dresses in black. And Bruce Springsteen, who was asked to record a tribute album to Seeger in 1997. In the end, he recorded but did not include the song that has surely influenced my life more than any other... it just asserted itself too forcefully among the others in his collection:

It's the hammer of justice
It's the bell of freedom
It's the song about the love between my brothers and my sisters
All over this land

No wonder Bono would be named Man of the Year by TIME magazine, for following Seeger's lyrical advice - and example. I have certainly tried to live my life in alignment to these lyrics.

Recently, Seeger was introduced at a "pro bono" school concert with these words: "He's probably the person who's done more for this country than anyone I can think of."

You need both spirituality and activism – Bible and almanac. Upon graduation from medical school, the members of the Med's Gospel Team all became medical missionaries. They headed for three continents - into Ecuador, Zambia and China. However, en route to China my father stopped in Europe to study tropical medicine. During that year (1949) the Bamboo Curtain came down and missionaries were no longer able to enter. So he diverted to the Belgian Congo, where I was born.

The principle that both groups shared is that all human beings are created equal. In the mid-20th century, this meant either you could either become a missionary or a socialist – Bible or almanac, I suppose. The medical missionaries exerted huge influence in remote parts of the Third World. Meanwhile, Seeger got called up before Congress's Un-American Activities Committee. For pleading the First Amendment (not the Fifth) he was indicted for contempt of Congress, but this was later overturned by an appeals court. Advocacy is seen by many as a higher calling than service provision, but it often comes at a cost in terms of your reputation. But having a bad reputation does not always mean that you lose your influence. Medical missionaries in countries that joined the Second World (communist bloc) often lost their reputation when they were called reactionaries, but this seldom diminished their influence.

Here is a story recorded by Alec Wilkinson in the New Yorker (April 17, 2006). It is told by a man named John Cronin, who is the director of the Pace Academy for the Environment, at Pace University. Cronin has known Seeger for thirty years. "About two winters ago, on Route 9 outside Beacon, one winter day, it was freezing – rainy and slushy, a miserable winter day – the war in Iraq is just heating up and the country's in a poor mood," Cronin said. "I'm driving north, and on the other side of the road, I see from the back a tall, slim figure in a hood and coat. I'm looking, and I can tell it's Pete. He's standing there all by himself, and he's holding up a big piece of cardboard that clearly has something written on it. Cars and trucks are going by him. He's getting wet. He's holding the homemade sign above his head – he's very tall, and his chin is raised the way he does when he sings – and he's turning the sign in a semi-circle, so that the drivers can see it as they pass, and some people are honking and waving at him, and some people are giving him the finger. He's eighty-four years old. I know he's got some purpose, of course, but I don't know what it is. What struck me is that, whatever his intentions are, and obviously he wants people to notice what he's doing, he wants to make an impression – anyway, whatever they are, he doesn't call the newspapers and say, "I'm Pete Seeger, here's what I'm going to do." He doesn't cultivate publicity. That isn't what he does. He's far more modest than that. He would never make a fuss. He's just standing out there in the cold and the sleet like a scarecrow. I go a little bit down the road, so that I can turn and come back, and when I get him in view again, this solitary and elderly figure, I see that what he's written on the sign is *Peace*."

Advocacy is legitimized by social activism. It is important to be out there, doing your part, not just speaking on talk shows and stuff. Which brings me to the purpose of writing these reflections. My father is almost as old as Pete Seeger, and he is still an activist too. Already in 2007 he has spent two months overseas, helping out his favorite cause. It was good to observe him back in a position of influence – helping to bring about intellectual and attitudinal change...

But best of all, for a career that has included both overseas and domestic health service, and for his example of serving others through faith-based organizations, he was awarded the Order of Canada this month. This is the highest civilian honor that can be bestowed on a citizen, and he deserves it.

This month also, TIME magazine released its annual issue containing the 100 most influential people in the world. I was wondering how many of those listed will have the staying power of these two personal heroes of mine - one who taught me to revere the Bible, and the other who wrote protest songs for the Almanac Singers? To love my neighbor, and to hammer out injustice. If only two of the 100 can do so, the world will be a better place for our grandchildren.

Bob Dylan

A rebel rebelling against the rebellion

In *Rolling Stone's* The 100 Greatest Artists of All Time, Bob Dylan is voted #2, second only to the Beatles. Robbie Robertson writes about him in that magazine... that he was "a rebel rebelling against the rebellion." Let me explain... When Bruce Springsteen inducted Dylan into the Rock 'n' Roll Hall of fame in 1988, he said: "Elvis freed our bodies and Dylan freed our minds". Elvis led the rebellion. Dylan rebelled against it.

Dylan deserves the Noble prize that he won this week. Let me explain again...

For one thing, he kept reinventing himself. He started as a folksinger and ended up as a rock star. He was iconic playing an acoustic guitar with a harmonica on a neck-stand, from 1961. When he first "went electric" at the 1965 Newport Folk Festival he got a mix of cheers and boo's – he divided his fans. This would happen time and again but he kept trending.

Think Andile Mngxitama. He is rebelling against the rebellion too. Julius Malema is the rebel who is rebelling. Andile is rebelling against the rebellion. We need them both. Juju is Elvis, the King. Andile is Dylan. He rejects the rebellion and offers you something purer.

With no disrespect meant to Julius, Andile offers something that derives from Fanon and Sebukwe like Dylan emerged in the line of Woodie Guthrie, Pete Seeger and Johnny Cash.

Then came a motorcycle accident followed by several reclusive years raising a family in upstate New York. Normalizing. But the musicians who played with them formed *The Band* and became so good themselves that they launched another great band into orbit.

This led Dylan into a country music period, heralded by the *Nashville Skyline* album. It starts with a duet with Johnny Cash, recorded on the King of Country's TV show. The one and only time that I saw him myself, live in concert, he played acoustic in the first half, inviting Joan Baez to join him about half-way through this set. Do you know what I mean when I say that you don't really appreciate the beauty of Dylan's music until you hear someone else sing it? Quintessentially Baez – but others too like Peter, Paul and Mary and so many more. Dylan's voice is unique – musically rustic. But you know what? He is rebelling against the rebellion and didn't want you to hear the music – *but the words*. Remember, he won the Nobel prize for *Literature*. If you turn off Dylan because you don't like his voice, then *you don't get it*.

After the intermission he went into electric guitar mode.

Then Dylan was born again. Yep, religiously speaking. Three consecutive albums and one whole tour were devoted to the gospel message. He didn't even sing his old hits in these concerts – once again dividing his fans. But he won a Grammy Award for the "best male rock vocal performance" of 1979 for the memorable song "Gotta Serve Somebody". This is my personal favorite Dylan song from my favorite album of all - Slow Train Comin'. I took him at his word. It changed my life:

> *It may be the Devil*
> *Or it may be the Lord*
> *But you gotta serve somebody*

The Band gave way to *Tom Petty and the Heartbreakers* for a number of years, then on to a *no-name band* (pun intended) for his "Never Ending Tour" – hired guns. Each time he reinvented himself, he shed some fans but these were replaced by new ones. I'm one of the lucky ones that liked each and every one of his reincarnations.

Then I got an idea. Why not paraphrase his most famous songs to try to get the message through to those two hard-headed denialists – Thabo Mbeki and his Health Minister (may her name be forgotten). Here are the best 3 lines, one from each of the 3 verses – that's why they don't rhyme:

1. *How many deaths will it take 'til she knows that too many people have died?*

2. *How many years can the nation exist before it is brought to its knees?*

3. *How many years can an orphan survive before someone gives him a hand?*

The answer, my friend, is a-groanin in the wind, the answer is groanin in the wind.

I recorded it under a sensible nome de plume – Robin Dylan. I even sent a courtesy copy to Zachie Achmat as a gift of thanks. Dylan is not a folksinger or a rock star. Dylan is a bard, a poet, even a prophet. He performed at a Roman Catholic youth festival in Bologna, Italy in 1997 before Pope John Paul II, who in his speech at the event described Christ as "the road a man must walk down before they call him a man".

Now hear this. In 1975, the unthinkable had happened... a President had just resigned... a war had been lost... causing what one of Dylan's biographers calls a "haze of meaninglessness". Does this sound familiar, or what?

That year Bob Dylan wrote a song called "Tangled Up in Blue". It is from what some consider the best album he ever released – *Blood on the Tracks*. Some also interpret the album as addressing the disintegration of marriage, for Dylan's first marriage had been on the rocks for a while and the split came soon after. This is also all-too-familiar, 40 years on. His memorable words were:

The only thing I knew how to do was to keep on keepin' on

There are two countries. One you can see in the news. People build fortunes and infrastructure. But in the singer's country they work as cooks, fishermen and dancers. Sadly, revolutionaries turn into drug dealers. But the singer keeps on traveling, unafraid and unfinished. It's prophetic advice.

Speaking about his private life, Dylan once said: "you can't be wise and in love at the same time".

Above all, Dylan epitomizes something that is democratic. Not just the freedom of speech, but the responsibility that non-government voices have to make democracy work. When during the Struggle the activists and marginalized sang *Umshini Wam*, it was rebels rebelling against the rebellion. The rebellion was Evolutionary change. When the poor, the have- nots, rebel against that fatalism and demand Revolutionary change, you get voices rebelling against the rebellion. It does not make democratic sense for the establishment to sing this song.

These are the days of Robbespierre. Bob Dylan deserves his Nobel prize and South Africa deserves no less than Equality. As he famously put it:

Any day now, any day now, I shall be released!

13. LIVING LEGENDS

IT'S been quite a week. Intriguing. At times moving. Quite remarkable.

Yesterday more than 100 world leaders attended the Mandela memorial along with 70 000 South Africans in a stadium that many associate with the 2010 soccer World Cup. Madiba worked so hard and so long to bring that tournament to Africa.

I will just share a few highlights of my reflections during this grieving process..

I saw Bill Clinton being interviewed. He and Mandela were concurrent presidents in their respective countries. They remained good friends. Both have strong Methodist roots.

Clinton said that he once got up the courage to ask Mandela if, as he famously walked out of those prison gates, he really didn't hate those people who kept him incarcerated for 27 years. He answered Clinton: "Briefly. But I knew that if I kept hating them, I would still be their prisoner. And I wanted to be *free*. So I let it go."

This says a lot to me about the nature of forgiveness. It is not only good for those we forgive. It is good for us. "Forgive us our trespasses, as we forgive those that trespass against us." At some stage, we need to let go of hate, and put the past behind us.

President Obama's eulogy yesterday was the best. He included a Mandela quote that has fascinated me: "I am not a saint, unless by that you mean a sinner who keeps trying." I resonate with this comment. For far too long I somehow associated the word "missionary" with the saints. But I myself am living proof that this is not so. But I do keep trying to contribute. At the end of my CV is my epitaph: "I came. I saw. I contributed." I am not a conqueror. Or a saint. But I am a missionary.

The third Mandela quote that has intrigued me is from the Treason Trials. Obama reminded us that this speech was at the time of Kennedy and Kruschev! "I have fought white domination and I have fought black domination." Years later, no, decades later, he was still fighting both. The main plot was of course ending white minority rule. But there were those who wanted to replace white domination with black domination. That was the sub- plot to the story, and we have to recognize Mandela's role on that front as well. His parting with Winnie could be construed in this light. He was President of all South Africans, and she had become embittered and radicalized. Mamphela Ramphele calls it "woundedness" - generically, I don't mean that she said that of Winnie specifically. Some people, no, many people, still can't get past "the past". Mandela's great spirituality stems from that one word in his reply to Clinton: "Briefly." He felt it... then he let it go.

By the way, the movie <u>Long Walk to Freedom</u> does Winnie a big favour - by putting her militant attitudes in context. She really suffered for the cause... in solitary confinement for over a year. A mother parted from her children. It's funny, many are quick to forgive her, who are slow to forgive and forget "the past". Mandela somehow managed to get above it all.

My mind keeps asking: *What is the difference between "black domination" and affirmative action that favours the large majority?*

That brings me back to another favorite theme and person... I see that <u>TIME</u> magazine has voted Pope Francis I to be *Person of the Year* for 2013. I second the emotion. Here's why, from an article by Mike Kohen this week called **Our country is still in white hands**:

"The stability that Mandela engineered in those early days after apartheid never made South Africa an economic dynamo. Economic growth has averaged 3.5% since 2004, compared with 10.5% in China.

"Moreover, the Gini coefficient, a measure of economic equality, has risen to 0.63 in 2009 from 0.59 in 1993, making South Africa one of the world's most unequal countries."

The risk to Mandela's legacy is that "inequality and exclusion" (to quote Pope Francis, again generically speaking) could *drain the gains*. In any country, regardless of the colour bar, poor people can come to resent the rich. Not always and not everywhere, depending to some extent on the local culture's comfort or discomfort with what Gerte Hofstede calls "power distance". But where the disparities are acute and glaring, it will breed discontent. Aristotle said that inequality is the mother of revolution.

Yes, there has to be redress, no question. But when is the cut-off point for affirmative action? Or will there ever be one, when the rich are getting richer and ranks of the poor are growing? Also, as the ranks of the rich include more and more "successful" blacks, is not a class system being created? Put another way, many poor people will not be in a forgiving mood, ready to forget "the past". So it is double-jeopardy for South Africa to let the "wealth gap" increase.

If you are rich by your own standards, the question is: *How much is enough?*

If you are "historically disadvantaged" and thus deserve positive discrimination, the question is: *How long should you have that advantage, before YOU end up with more than enough?*

Thinking Locally, Acting Globally

For non-South Africans, the example of Nelson Mandela is also relevant. For in his own rural poor context, he was also privileged – from the royal family, getting early exposure to leadership role models and an education. After urbanizing, he became a professional, a lawyer, and co-owned a law firm with Oliver Tambo. So he was (relatively) well off, although among the oppressed. Even in prison, he was a *political* prisoner, not a criminal.

The point is, look what he did with the few advantages he enjoyed. I was reduced to tears this week when Mac Maharaj, a co-prisoner at Robben Island, described how Mandela would sometimes be served better food than the other prisoners because of the esteem that even his jailers had for him. Like bread, when everyone else got only pap. He would call over other prisoners, especially the younger ones, and share it with them, recognizing the deprivation that they faced because of a shared cause.

We need to apply the biblical principles that are there in the Old Testament Poor Laws – sabbath, sabbatical, Jubilee... to keep levelling the playing field. This has to be continuous. Pope Francis is right that money can end up being a form of idolatry, like the Golden Calf.

My Privilege

If he was still alive... today would be Madiba's 100th birthday.

Obama gave a stirring lecture this week in Joburg - the Nelson Mandela Memorial Lecture. It is an annual event. He aimed his remarks obliquely at Trump.

While Mandela was still incarcerated, I became more aware of him and how important an icon he was for *The Struggle*. I prayed for him every day for YEARS, no kidding. I was worshipping in an Anglican church at that time, in Canada. Sometimes the minister would invite extemporaneous prayer from "the pews". I would pray for Mandela and ask God for his release. I think my teenage kids were a bit embarrassed by this at the time?

After this happened several times, one of the parishioners came up to me in the foyer after a service, when everyone was putting on their coats and boots to face the winter cold. "Who is Nelson Mandela?" they asked curiously, prompted by my repeated prayer.

My reply even surprised me - maybe it was a word of prophecy? "He is the future President of South Africa" I blurted out, adding: "but he is still in prison." At that time the Berlin Wall was still standing, but some of us could see that neither Communism nor Apartheid were gonna make it.

I can only add that 30 years later, I am now not sure that Capitalism is going to make it!

Thomas Sankara

In the language of the old Upper Volta, the words "Burkina Faso" mean: "Land of upright men". The country was re-named this by Africa's Ché Guevara, a young leader called Thomas Sankara.

This highlights his idealism. He was also creative... an accomplished guitarist, he also wrote Burkina Faso's new national anthem. He said a week before he was assassinated: "While revolutionaries as individuals can be murdered, you cannot kill ideas." He was right. His actions were stopped, but his ideas, idealism, creativity and innovation live on.

He was a military man, so when a military government was formed in Upper Volta in 1981, Sankara got his first taste of governance - as Secretary of State for Information. He rode to his first cabinet meeting on a bicycle! But he resigned the next year when he perceived the regime's anti-labour drift.

These were turbulent times with various failed and successful coups, but two years later, Sankara became President at the age of 33. The ideology of his Revolution was defined as anti-imperialist. He spoke in forums like the Organization for African Unity against what he described as neo-colonialist penetration of Africa through Western trade and finance. He called for a united front of African nations to repudiate their foreign debt.

Here are some of the actions that validated his words and ideas for Change. They merit recollection (from Wikipedia):

- He refused to use the air conditioning in his office on the grounds that such luxury was not available to anyone but a handful
- As President, he lowered his salary to $450 a month and limited his possessions to a car, four bikes, three guitars, a fridge and a broken freezer
- A motorcyclist himself, he formed an all-women motorcycle personal guard

- He was known for jogging unaccompanied through the capital in his track suit and posing in his tailored military fatigues
- When asked why he didn't want his portrait hung in public places, as was the norm for other African leaders, he replied "There are seven million Thomas Sankaras"
- He sold off the government fleet of Mercedes cars and made the Renault (the cheapest car sold in Burkina Faso at that time) the official service car of the ministers
- He reduced the salaries of well-off public servants, including his own, and forbade the use of government chauffeurs and 1st class airline tickets
- He forced well-off civil servants to pay one month's salary to public projects
- He required public servants to wear a traditional tunic, woven from Burkinabe cotton and sewn by Burkinabe craftsmen
- In Ouagadougou, Sankara converted the army's provisioning store into a state- owned supermarket open to everyone (the first supermarket in the country)
- He redistributed land from the feudal landlords to the peasants. Wheat production increased from 1700 kg per hectare to 3800 kg per hectare
- His government banned female genital mutilation, forced marriages and polygamy; while appointing females to high governmental positions and encouraging them to work outside the home and stay in school even if pregnant

South Africa is experiencing some political earthquakes. The tectonic plates are shifting, causing a future Labour Party to appear on the horizon. Organized labour is restless, uncomfortable in the ruling alliance. This is the second split – between Left and Neo- liberals. Another split has already emerged – *along age lines*. A new party called the Economic Freedom Fighters is the first one ever to be basically youth-led.

Sankara was consistent. How can you expect the working class and largely unemployed youth both to support a government that has gone mad in terms of waste and graft?

How can a government that ignores Corruption and spends billions that it can't give account for (according to the Auditor General) to be a force for Economic Emancipation?

Pope Francis I

One observer offered the following 19 reasons why he felt that Pope Francis I deserves the accolade as Man of the Year. I have left the 11 things he did in normal font, and put in italics *things he said* to bring his influence to bear on Change. (This sometimes called public engagement or advocacy.)

1. He spoke out against frivolous spending by the Church
2. He invited a boy with Downs Syndrome for a ride in the Popemobile
3. He embraced and kissed a man badly scarred by a genetic skin disease
4. *He denounced the judgment of homosexuals*
5. He held a major ceremony at the chapel of a youth prison, and washed their feet
6. *He urged the protection of the Amazon Rainforest*
7. He personally called and consoled a victim of rape
8. He snuck out of the Vatican to feed the homeless
9. He auctioned his motorcycle to benefit the homeless
10. *He acknowledged that atheists can be good people*
11. *He condemned the global financial system*
12. *He fought child abuse*
13. *He condemned the violence of the Syrian civil war*
14. He redirected employee bonuses to charity

15. *He spoke out against the Church's 'obsession' with abortion, gay marriage and contraception*
16. *He called for cooperation between Christians and Muslims*
17. He took part in a selfie
18. He invited homeless men to his birthday meal
19. He refused to send away a child who had run on stage to hug him

Our deeds or actions validate our words. The reverse is also true. That is, when leaders actually steal from the public purse, or waste resources, or think of their own benefits first with little regard for the plight of those who elected them, then no one listens to them. Thousands of years ago, Lao Tzu put it this way: *"A leader is best when people barely know that he exists. Not so good when people obey and acclaim him, worse when they despise him. Fail to honour people, they fail to honour you; but of a good leader, who talks little, when his work is done, his aim fulfilled, they will all say, 'We did this ourselves.'"*

14. CHANGE AGENTS

Ahmed Kathrada

"AK" was the youngest of the Treason Trialists. So he out-lived most of them, and thus it was finally left to him to write a letter to a State President, asking him to resign. This he did only a year or so before his own passing.

"AK" was also one of the ANC Stalwarts, but as Party structures, the Veterans and Stalwarts are really part of governance. So they are not "non-state institutions", but rather a case of the party talking to itself.

In fact, one MP from that party is Chairperson of the Ahmed Kathrada Foundation - Derek Hanekom. After he was dumped as a Minister, he said that he would not be deterred from speaking out, by letters threatening to discipline him. Hanekom said government had lost an estimated R100 billion through Gupta projects.

The core focus of the Ahmed Kathrada Foundation is "deepening non-racialism". Finding this racial rapprochement is mission-critical to finding solutions to inequality and unemployment – without losing the rule of law.

In Ahmed Kathrada's *Memoirs*, Edwin Markham is quoted:
He drew a circle to shut me out heretic, rebel, a thing to flout
But Love and I had the wit to win
We drew a circle that took him in

Mogoeng Mogoeng

Mogoeng was born on 14 January 1961 in Goo-Mokgatha village near Zeerust in the North West Province. His father was a miner and his mother a domestic worker. Mogoeng became politically active at high school, from which he was briefly suspended for organising a memorial to the victims of the Soweto uprising.

Top Judge in the Top Court

He has now been appointed to preside over the Constitutional Court. In his public addresses he has been "outspoken" and "forthright". He has regularly championed judicial independence and deplored interference by the Executive Branch.

Mogoeng is a lay preacher in the Pentecostal Winners' Chapel. He attributed the criticism over his nomination and appointment to his Christian faith. But in Mogoeng's view, stated at his JSC interview, God wanted him to be Chief Justice.

Like Nathan of old, the prophet who critiqued King David, albeit in a different context and structure, Mogoeng Mogoeng has proven that he has the courage *to speak truth to power*.

Public Protectors

The writers of South Africa's Constitution deemed it necessary not only to constitute a Judiciary, but also these ombudswomen-and-men. Busisiwe Mkhwebane and her predecessor Thuli Madonsela have very different styles. But their role in the "mother-of-all-Section-9-institutions" is critical to Democracy.

The PR system (i.e. proportional representation) has left Members of Parliaments (MPs) in a quandary about how exactly (and how best) to exercise their constitutional Oversight role. Thus this extra slate of Section 9 institutions has helped to maintain the balance of powers.

The Legislative branch can create conditions for the Section 9 institutions to be heard. The office of the Public Protector is required to appear before the National Assembly at least once every year. During Madonsela's budget and strategic presentations, the advocate was requested to present progress reports before Parliament on a quarterly basis.

The Executive branch has at times challenged reports prepared by the Public Protector. Ex-President Zuma attempted to interdict the

State of Capture report from being made public. Soon after that, Madonsela's completed her term of office. But Mkhwebane said she would block any attempt to sideline her predecessor's recommendation by arguing that the matter warrants a judicial review. More recently, Mkhwebane has challenged the next President, Cyril Ramaphosa, on the legality of donations to his "CR-17" campaign to become party leader. Painful as this is for them both, transparency must be guarded at all costs.

Other state institutions have challenged the Public Protector as well, like the Reserve Bank - which won a case in court to have Mkhwebane's recommendations set aside. (The RB is another section 9 institution.) In some minds this raises questions about her fitness for service, and erodes the high moral ground that she is supposed to stand on.

Father Stanislaus Mayibe

This Dominican Father was the first citizen to file a complaint about "State Capture" with the Public Protector. When prudent church leaders speak out like this, it is a prophetic voice.

Catholic Commission of Justice and Peace

Father Mayibe works at this church institution which is an Advocacy arm of the church.

Just as prophecy can be an "office" as in the OT prophets who were not Levites or priests, so it can be a spiritual "gift" of ordinary, caring Christians who sense that they should speak up when they see an injustice. Some churches like ZCC hold prophets in high esteem, along with pastors and bishops.

15. KEEPERS

Nombuyisela Noah

In his autobiography <u>Born a Crime</u>, Trevor Noah tells this anecdote:

"Obviously, I was not the only child born to black and white parents during apartheid. Travelling around the world today, I meet other mixed South Africans all the time. Our stories start off identically. We're around the same age. Their parents met at some underground party in Hillbrow or Cape Town. They lived in an illegal flat. The difference is that in virtually every other case they left. The white parent smuggled them out through Lesotho or Botswana, and they grew up in exile, in England or Germany or Switzerland, because being a mixed family under apartheid was just that unbearable.

"Once Mandela was elected we could finally live freely. Exiles started to return. I met my first one when I was around seventeen. He told me his story, and I was like, "Wait, what? You mean we could have left? That was an option?" Imagine being thrown out of an airplane. You hit the ground and break all your bones, you go to hospital and you heal and you move on and finally put the whole thing behind you – and then one day somebody tells you about parachutes. That's how I felt. I couldn't understand why we'd stayed. I went strait home and asked my mom.

"Why? Why didn't we just leave? Why didn't we go to Switzerland?"

"Because I am not Swiss," she said, as stubborn as ever. "This is my country. Why should I leave?"

Indeed. My sentiments exactly. I have failed forward. I have learned. I can now start again - better informed. Why should I leave? I like it here.

Why do I include Nombutisela Noah as a keeper?

First, it brings Book 2 right up to the present. Krotoa was long ago, followed by the pioneer missionaries of the LMS, and Tiyo Soga was then about half-way to the present. But Nombutisela is my contemporary. Second, because she too entered a mixed marriage, of sorts, to father a child. Third, because that child has grown up to be a household word, and this gives a ring of truth to Book 2 and goes straight to its *relevance*.

She loved her country, but defied it. She loved her son, but put him in harm's way. She loved her son's father, but her sons were *her own project*.

Nombutisela Noah's mother (i.e. Trevor's grandmother) urbanized from the Eastern Cape to Johannesburg. This was the same trajectory as Nelson Mandela, and not long after him: *"My whole family is religious, but where my mother was Team Jesus all the way, my grandmother balanced her Christian faith with the traditional Xhosa beliefs she'd grown up with, communicating with the spirits of our ancestors..."*

Nombutisela brought her two boys up well: *"The only music I knew was from church: soaring, uplifting songs praising Jesus. It was the same with movies. My mom didn't want my mind polluted by movies with sex and violence. So the Bible was my action movie. Samson was my superhero. He was my He-Man. A guy beating a thousand people to death with the jawbone of a donkey? That's pretty badass..."*

Reading Trevor Noah's accounts of growing up with a Swiss-German father who lived in another apartment down the hall from his mom, and the way this illegal arrangement played out on the streets is both hilarious and chilling. She took her two sons to several churches every Sunday in a circuit, as well as to mid-week events:

"In Soweto, religion filled the void left by absent men...

"Their fathers were off working in a mine somewhere, able to come home only during the holidays. Their fathers had been sent to prison. Their fathers were in exile, fighting for the cause..."

"I used to ask my mom if it was hard for her to raise me alone without a husband. She'd reply, "Just because I live without a man doesn't mean I've never had a husband. God is my husband." For my mom, my aunt, my grandmother, and all other women on our street, life centred on faith."

Relevance

At this point in time, you cannot separate South Africa and Christianity. Blaming it on missionaries is a bit pointless now, it is a done deal.

The church is also very influential still in society. For example, the first complaint filed with the Public Protector about State Capture was submitted by a Dominican priest, Father Stanislaus Mayibe. Soon after that, in Soweto, the South African Council of Churches released the report of its Unburdening Panel. It severely implicated political leaders at the highest levels. Even the Anglican archbishop has called on the President to step down, in the feisty tradition of his predecessor Desmond Tutu

By far the largest church denomination in South Africa today is the ZCC (Zion Christian Church). Churches like these are "owned and run" by Africans for mostly Africans. I have visited Moria twice – once to the Bird side and the other to the Star side. On the first occasion, I was seeking advice from a prophet about what to do about a thorny situation in my life. I remember his few words, as he lay on a mat and prayed for me. They were very, very close to the mark.

Did I mention that historically the Zion in ZCC does not refer to the mountain in the Levant where Jerusalem is located, but to a town in Michigan? It is the town where the missionaries came from, to train local leaders. When their work was done, they returned to the USA leaving the church they established to run itself. It has expanded into a massive church denomination.

It is not right to call this phenomenal rise of Christianity "cultural genocide". Church leaders in South Africa moves comfortably with Muslim, Hindu, Buddhist and traditional faith leaders. There is no intolerance, nor is anyone coerced – the church blesses them, serves them and looks out for their best interests. Ask Nombutisela Noah!

Christianizing Africa and Africanizing Christianity

The Christian religion started as a "splinter" of Judaism in the Levant, in New Testament times. The first wave of missionaries – the Twelve Apostles - fanned out in all directions. Because Rome was the super-power at that time, the centre of gravity of the church moved from the Levant to Rome. But you still have churches founded by the apostles that are not Roman – in Syria, Iraq, Ethiopia, Egypt, Greece, Armenia, Russia and India.

Roman Catholic missionaries went on to convert the peoples of France, Holland and Germany. Thence to England, Ireland and Scandinavia. From northern Europe, later, came Protestantism. The Counter-Reformation followed, sending missionaries like the Jesuits all over the world during the Age of Discovery. On the heels of that wave came the "modern missionary movement" featured in this book. Emphasis was shifting again to mass literacy/education and health. In the later stages came development and economic empowerment. In sheer numbers, there are many more Christians today in the South than in the North. It is thus intellectually dishonest to call Christianity a "white man's religion". Jesus himself was not Caucasian. (Anti-Semitism became a scourge of racism because Jews are not Aryans.)

Also, church structure has adapted as it has migrated and moved on. There are places like Nubia where it has faded away. Today it is shrinking in Iraq at an alarming rate – centuries after it was established. It has had flat institutional structures and tall ones – congregational and episcopal. The Anti-Slavery movement arose from "non-conformist" churches. Pastors like Tiyo Soga trended the church into ecumenical, inter-denominational linkages. The space this created allowed room for the African-initiated churches to arise.

South African citizens know all this, instinctively. Mama Noah is one of those who can tell you.

I salute you, Nombutisela! Go with God. Long live another black Queen!

Mohamed Bouazizi and Andries Tekane

Tomorrow is Freedom Day. This bulletin is about two African youth, one Muslim, one Christian... freedom fighters.

Has anybody here seen my old friend Bouazizi? Can you tell me where he's gone?

He inspired a lot of people, it seems the good, they die young
I just turned around and he's gone!

In the latest issue of <u>The Thinker</u>, Dr. Essop Pahad waxes eloquent about Tunisia:

"Tunisia is an African country. Its glorious history of Carthage and Hannibal is part of our African heritage... Tunisia was one of the first countries in Africa, in 1956, to wrest its political independence from France. It is one of the founding members of the OAU and later the AU. Now, 55 years after that glorious event in our continent, Africa should take pride in the heroic actions of the people of Tunisia.

"An unemployed university graduate Mohamed Bouazizi is harassed, assaulted, humiliated and forcibly prevented from earning a meager income by selling fruits and vegetables. In desperation and in an action of defiance he sets himself on fire. This act of self-immolation triggered demonstrations by his family in Sidi Bouzid. They were joined by hundreds of people, mainly young, in their protests. Very rapidly this demonstration spread like wild-fire throughout the country and eventually brought down the President.

"This young hero, Mohamed Bouazizi, will forever be credited with inspiring the overthrow of the 23-year old regime of Zine al-Abidine Ben Ali. Under this regime Tunisia had been lauded and fêted as a very successful, wealthy, fast-growing economy; and according to an IMF report

it was the "most competitive economy in Africa" and ranked 40th in the world.

"Progressive organizations and individuals, including journalists, were subject to arbitrary arrest, detention and torture. This iron-fisted rule was the bedrock of an economy that spawned massive inequality between rich and poor, high unemployment rates, including many jobless university graduates, ever-increasing prices of basic commodities and a serious lack of any form of redistribution...

"The developments in Tunisia are earth-shattering. They have had a massive impact, for the good, in Egypt, Algeria, Jordan, Yemen and other countries in Africa and the Middle East.

Mohamed Bouazizi and the other martyrs did not die in vain. Whatever happens, Tunisia will never be the same. The democratic process cannot be halted, neo-colonialism has suffered a huge blow and autocratic regimes in Africa and the Middle East are feeling the heat. However, the forces of neo-colonialism and monopoly capital may still take advantage of current instability to push for the establishment of new governments sympathetic to their interests, thus threatening the independence of these countries and the democratic rights of their people."

The problem with Colonialism was foreign interference. The Ben Ali regime was independent, so no one intervened - while people were denied their freedom. Is booming economic growth reason enough for the hands-off approach to human rights abuses? What does that say about what matters most?

The last C4L Bulletin contained the sad news of another death, another sacrifice, another young African who wanted a better deal for the poor.

Has anybody here seen my old friend Tatane? Can you tell me where he's gone?

He mobilized a lot of people, it seems the good, they die young I just turned around and he's gone!

Disparity in South Africa is phenomenal. Driving along the R21 highway this week from Pretoria to Joburg, I observed so many huge mansions sprouting up on the hill by Irene Mall, then within minutes the sprawling township of Tembisa. It is graphic to the point of being shocking. Someone described South Africa as a First World Country and a Third World Country occupying the same space.

But the same is true in global terms! This week I also retuned to Africa from Europe – it's just as graphic. Is anyone "free" in a society or a world like that?

Andries Tatane was on the right track. There is a *Myth of Spontaneous Development*. It doesn't just happen, it gets kick-started – by facilitation, activism and resources. In fact "intervention" actually means that someone has to "come between". So Tatane was out there, protesting the lack of service delivery. There are risks in being a freedom fighter.

It has often been said that if you are not part of the solution, then you are part of the problem. If our convictions and values allow us to stand by and watch while people's rights are denied, then we are guilty of passivism, maybe even fatalism. Ouch! Not everyone is a volunteer, but Voluntarism offers so many diverse ways to get involved.

In the days when there were still Second World Countries (the Communist Bloc as these were also called) there used to be dissidents and occasionally, defectors. Then Alexander Solzhenitsyn started writing books about the Gulag... then *glasnost*... then *perestroika*... and a New World Order. Migration is now booming – causing a brain drain for Africa.

Earlier cries of *Uhuru!* (freedom) turned to *Amandla!* (power) under Apartheid. The Struggle was not just for liberation but for empowerment. Now the question is being raised whether BEE (black economic empowerment) is going over the top? Pallo Jordan once wrote that the purpose of affirmative action was to create circumstances in which affirmative action would no longer be needed. It is a means, not an end. But there are concerns that it is becoming a destination, not just a journey - a permanent feature of the landscape. Will the time come when the adjective "positive" will dropped from in front of "discrimination". Does it dignify people to be selected by that criteria, and not competency?! Is entitlement "freedom"?

16. CURRENT EVENTS

Brexit

British history is very long. The Romans were there and Londondinium was already a busy place even before the time of Christ. One emperor – Hadrian – built a wall to keep out the Scots. Donald Trump was not the first to think of doing that. But perhaps the first major story affecting Britain's fortunes was the Roman exit from Britain. That was historic.

Then came invasions of the Angles and the Saxons – from Germany. The language of Olde English is the same as Old German.

Then the Vikings powered up and parts of England were ruled by the Danes.

But the second major story in British history was the Norman invasion in 1066. For a long time after that, England and France combined into one nation, divided by the English channel. So the German influence started to fade as a lot of French crept in. Soon this creole of German and French hardened into a new language called English. It was later carried across the ocean along with other languages like Spanish, French and German, but English prevailed in North America. Mostly. In many dialects. Leading George Bernard Shaw to comment that England and America are two countries separated by the same language!

It is somehow ironic that the European Union has a single currency but nations have kept their respective languages. Salzburg is said to now have more translators than diplomats. The EU is not a melting pot like the United States, although Spanish-creep is now a fact of life in North America.

The third major news story must have been the signing of the Magna Carta. There was this emerging tug-of-war between the "divine right of kings" (ruling by decree) and consultation with citizens through their representatives. This would take centuries to perfect, but it was the dawn of Democracy in Britain.

Perhaps the fourth major story in British history was the defeat of the Spanish Armada? By this time, Spain had become the super-power of the world, and England was only in its adolescence. This maritime defeat set England on its way to a long era in which *Britannia ruled the waves*. In due course this made possible an Empire on which the sun never set – all around the world. Genghis Khan had ruled the largest land empire in history, but his sea campaigns to Japan and Java fizzled out. Whereas the British Empire was connected by the seven seas.

The fifth major story was the invasion of William of Orange from Holland. Yes it was a military invasion, but he was basically welcomed by Londoners in exchange for a deposed king who was messing around with parliament again. William had the good prudence to decline being crowned just because of a military victory. He asked that parliament be re- convened, and invite him to rule. This was the basis of a definitive rapprochement between royalty and parliament – an unwritten Constitution.

Now to make a long story short, the sixth major story was the Battle of Britain. Since the invasions of the Saxons, the Danes and the Normans, England had not really been invaded again. The Spanish had tried and failed. Well, OK, William came over from Holland but he was married to the defeated king's sister, so it was really by invitation that he landed. Hitler decided to give it a go in 1940, but was repelled. *"Never was so much owed by so many to so few"* was the way Winston Churchill described Britain's air superiority. The threat of German invasion was repelled.

And surely the emergence of a common market first, followed by a common currency and the European Union, was a huge news story. The seventh major news story is that Britain agreed to join in, well sort of - while keeping its own currency. It wanted to see the EU succeed, but was never sure that it fit. This wobbling has gone on for forty years, in an era when population growth has taken off and current events are covered by instant, global media.

It is not an exaggeration to put Brexit alongside these other seven defining trendings in British history. On its own, the UK will have the fifth largest economy in the world, and plenty of linkages – to the Continent, to the Commonwealth, and to America.

The media is treating Brexit like just another news story. It's not. It is monumental. It is an earthquake. It is more than historical, it is awesome. Whichever way it pans out, there is once again that feeling that *so many will owe it to so few* – that is, to the negotiating team. They are pulling off a huge shake-up... diplomatically. Without military confrontation.

The majority voted for Brexit. In a Democracy, the majority should rule. When Solon of Athens invented Democracy, his sense was that the only way that military power, or the oligarchy, or despots could be overpowered, was by Majority rule. He was onto something. We are now watching history in the making, peacefully, publicly and professionally. On TV, in the comfort of our living room. There is progress as human history moves forward.

The Parable of the Candle

Kingdonomics is like a lady who came to the kitchen around dusk to prepare supper for her family. She had noted on her cell-phone that there would be load-shedding at 7 p.m. She could not finish cooking and serve them by then, but she could have supper prepared and cooking on the stove.

As a precaution, she lit a candle. So that when the lights went out from the power cut, she would still be able to see what she was doing. But due to the heat of the candle, the stove, the kettle and the toaster, the kitchen windows started to steam up.

So she opened the kitchen window wide, to ventilate the kitchen while she worked and to defrost the windows. But the candle then started to flicker wildly and then went out.

She adjusted the window and re-lit the candle. Just then, the electric lights went out. She needed both the light of the candle and the window ventilation. Thank God that she had a gas stove, she thought. So she only opened the window part way. When there were gusts of wind she closed it a little more. The candle illuminated the kitchen and the windows defrosted. Supper was ready on time, in spite of the load-shedding.

In this parable, the candle is the guidance of Scripture when the big lights of capitalism or socialism fail us. And they do, at different times and in different ways. The light of Kingdonomics is enough to proceed with our life and work. It is sustainable although fragile.

But when we open wide the window, or close it, we experience the extremes. In South Africa, the rush of wind of the Alt-Right can quickly blow out the candle, leaving us in the dark. Or when we close the window tight, we fog up with the hot air of Leftist populism and ethnic hate-speech.

Leaving the window open enough to get ventilation but without blowing out the candle of Kingdonomics is a centrist solution. It is a mixed economy that includes both forces but lets neither force become dominant. Every election is an adjustment of how wide we leave the window open. That depends of the external wind and weather, and the internal conditions as we live and work.

Yes there are bigger lights - when there is electricity or sunlight. But at times these fail or fade and we need to keep the candle of Kingdonomics burning.

Thy word is a lamp unto my feet, and a light unto my path

During the rise of populism in the USA under Donald Trump (driven by his unprecedented use of Twitter) and also the concurrent Brexit delays in the UK, I noted that politics seemed to be polarizing. Later I heard that Davos 2020 named Polarization as one of the world's three biggest problems this year. A book was even published around that time called Why We're Polarized. In it, Ezra Klein wrote: "We are a collection of functional parts whose efforts combine into a dysfunctional whole."

Two of my close friends of many years have been very supportive to me, and yet they are poles apart in terms of politics in Canada, the USA and Europe. I found myself feeling pulled apart by opposing views, though I know them both to be fine Christians.

Then I connected the dots in the 2019 elections in South Africa. Parties at both extremes (Alt Right and populist Left) increased their numbers of seats in parliament – at the expense of both "centrist" parties. (We have a centre/left and a centre/right party.)

This takes you deeper into how the democratic systems work. More and more voices are saying that when people don't vote, or don't even register to vote, they are really "withdrawing their consent". They are opting out – voting with their feet; leaving Democracy behind in disappointment. Of an Electorate of 37 million last year, 18 million voted and 19 million stayed away.

The answer to this is to *fix the systems*. To reduce polarization, we need to reduce the populism and the partisanship and look for ways to bring people together. The Rev Jesse Jackson put it this way: "Leadership has a harder job to do than just choose sides. It must bring sides together."

EPILOGUE

Viva Contentment, Gratitude and Moderation!

There was a time when these three qualities were extolled as virtues. Today other forces are displacing them – like entitlement, consumerism and over-exuberance. So we hear of "lifestyle audits" and even spending ceilings to keep leaders from setting a bad example. In Canada, when Tommy Douglas was premier, he drove a Dodge – not a Cadillac. In Burkina Faso, Thomas Sankara made the Renault 5 the official car of cabinet ministers, to reduce expenditure on Mercedes limos. In the past year, Pope Francis has stated that leaders should drive "humble cars". He has declined to move into the Vatican Palace and is leading by example. Actions speak louder than words.

On my recent trip to Canada, the Premier of Alberta had to resign for making extravagant plans for a penthouse suite at the top of a government building. The planning did not follow normal channels. In South Africa, this is exactly what happened at Nkandla. Yet here the President's party did not ditch him, as hers did in Alberta, in spite of very clear outcomes of an investigation done by the ombudsman known as the Public Protector.

Contentment

Consumerism is the more modern, North American version of Capitalism. It is quite different from the older European version, in which wealth accumulated tended to be re- invested rather than spent. In fact, Consumerism was resisted in Europe at first, in the post- war years. It was regarded as gauche. But it prevailed. In this version, people are encouraged to be spenders not savers. The medium for this is called Marketing. How can Marketing work where there is contentment, gratitude and moderation?

The chickens have come home to roost. According to Sampie Terreblanche, it was high levels of consumer debt and government deficits led to the global economic slow-down that he calls the Great Recession (from 2008). He links this to both bail-outs of companies that were "too large to fail" and to an increase in corruption and corporate criminality. Again on my recent trip to Canada, I found that scandals in politics are not just a South African phenomenon!

Terreblanche writes: "The ideologies of neoliberal globalism and market fundamentalism that were sold so triumphantly – and arrogantly – to South Africa by the Americans in the early 1990s now stand thoroughly discredited." (p 35, Lost in Transformation).

I am a missionary not an economist. But on both sides of the Atlantic, I would like to see more redistribution of wealth – poor people living with more and rich people living with less. In South Africa, the legacy of neoliberalism is inequality. Some people have become fabulously wealthy, while most people have not felt an improvement in their lifestyle. This imbalance needs to be corrected... there is just no question about it.

Gratitude

The gospel of neoliberalism, brought to you by Ronald Reagan and Maggie Thatcher, said that lowering taxes would stimulate economic growth. Business would experience that "my cup runneth over" – and that would cause plenty of "trickle-down". This is where the nonprofit sector comes into Democracy. It is there to carry social benefits on through what in South Africa is called CSI (Corporate Social Investment). In this way companies express their gratitude to society by having a double bottom line – financial and social. They fund registered NGOs to provide care to the marginalized – those who fall through the cracks of the economy - like the unemployed and the destitute.

Pope Francis pointed out that the problem with this approach is *that they keep making the cup bigger*! His metaphor is instructive. Neither do I see it as only governments that do this, slowing the trickle-down effect. Certainly governments in the North rarely meet their pledges for development assistance, and public servants live on a gravy train where ever you go.

Sharing wealth with others is but a way of expressing thanks for what you have received. A good example is the Giving Pledge, but it is for millionaires, not for ordinary people. Do we give enough, as families and individuals? Or is our generosity diminished by the environment of Marketing, that drives people away from the values of contentment, gratitude and moderation? I have a sense that in the context of Consumerism, there has been a lot of drift from those virtues, and that each of us has a role in making the cup bigger, and thus reducing the trickle-down. This applies to prosperous South Africans living in a country where disparity is phenomenal – and to those overseas in "the West" whose lifestyles may become an issue to the Great Shepherd when he returns to separate the sheep from the goats.

Moderation

The ancient Stoics espoused this virtue. It was not Pope Francis who thought it up. The Lausanne covenant promotes the slogan: *Live simply so that others can simply live.*

C4L has scaled down for its own reasons – not so much there is less trickle-down, but because it recognized that it was living beyond its means. This caused it to go chasing after funding not so much to carry out its mission as to keep the wheels turning.

Some people may see this as slowdown or even failure. We don't. We see it as a sign of the times. How can we point the finger at government "fat cats" in our Advocacy programming when we ourselves are not ready to redistribute our wealth, especially for the cause that we champion – youth unemployment?

There is a difference between your income and your wealth. One is your personal Profit and Loss Statement for a month or a year. The other is your personal Balance Sheet. Most people gauge their giving by their income - for example, by tithing ten percent of it. But if you earn 100 000 per year, live on 50 000 and tithe 10 000, then you "store" 40 000 away in investments. You accumulate wealth by doing this year after year. What about deploying ten percent of your *wealth* for development, as well as ten percent of your income? That would make the cup smaller, and increase the trickle-down. We all need to do more, because the gap is getting wider as the trickle-down dries up.

Did you love *Opa Waxes Prophetic*? Then you should read *Rich Man, Poor Woman, Bogyman, Thief*[1] by CO Stephens and William O'Dowda!

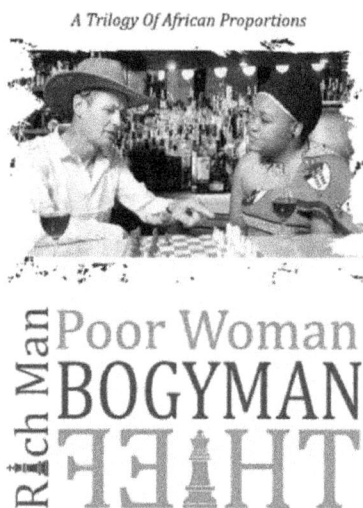

A Trilogy Of African Proportions

Rich Man Poor Woman BOGYMAN THIEF

WILLIAM O'DOWDA

2

The title has a familiar poetic ring to it. It is the second half of a rhyme that goes back to 1475, when William Caxton wrote a book about games The Game and Playe of the Cheese. It was a divination game, about who you were going to marry. Then AA Milne recycled it in 1927, in Now We Are Six. It is a playful turn of phrase, but serious too. So it is both traditional and relevant, like the book, which has recycled "beggar man" as "bogyman", to fit the narrative. And for gender balance, "poor man" has changed to "poor woman"... in keeping with the times.

Book 1 is the baseline narrative – a true story about someone who wasn't true. One reviewer of this book Black Queen White King Check

1. https://books2read.com/u/b5ZaOR

2. https://books2read.com/u/b5ZaOR

Mate wrote: "It is a cautionary tale, and it would be maudlin and tacky if it were not so interesting and well written." It exposes core themes of ancient versus modern, human rights versus the rights of the collective, and civil versus criminal.

Book 2 continues the narrative and then gets deep into issues related to customary marriage. This is very relevant in Africa, where most marriages by far adhere to these ancient customs. Which were shared by patriarchs like Isaac and Rebecca, Ruth and Boaz, right up to the late great rapper HHP and his "ex". All the way to the Supreme Court of Appeal in 2020 - disputing whether their customary marriage was valid or not. His family says that all the rites were not completed. Whereas she claims that because they lived together for three years, she has a right to his estate. Do gender rights trump aboriginal rights?

White King is Dead, Long Live Black Queen also revisits three historic inter-racial marriages, from Krotoa of the Sandlopers to Trever Noah's parents. Quoting the book reviewer again: "This is a fascinating look at South Africa through the eyes of a foreigner who has really made an effort to learn more than the average South Africa (black or white) knows about things."

Book 3 get positively controversial (pun intended). Friendly Fire in the Catherdral uses the issue of "HIV endangerment" as a litmus test, to discern whether the bride was ever sincere. If she wasn't, she was similar to the two South African's who tested positive early in the coronavirus crisis, who then "jumped quarantine" in KwaZulu-Natal. They were tracked down by contact-tracing, arrested, and charged with attempted murder. This books re-visits pestilences past, from the Black Plague right up to Covid-19, and applies lessons learned to the baseline narrative.

The author concludes that HIV endangerment may be over-criminalized in some settings, such as the HIV and AIDS pandemic in North America. In that context, it was viewed mainly as a sexually transmitted disease, mainly in the Gay community, and thus acquired double-jeopardy in terms of stigmatization. Whereas in

Africa is was much like Covid-19, knowing no boundaries of male, female, rich, poor, black, white, national or foreigner. In this context, HIV endangerment is a crime. But it is one that has been rarely prosecuted, because gender rights seem to trump victim rights. Even when it may have been weaponized to snafu the groom's estate.

The trilogy is autobiographical, written under a nome de plume to keep it as generic and informative as possible.

About the Publisher

Mbokodo Publishers is your choice service provider and partner in the publishing business. We make your business our business in order to understand your needs, tastes and challenges better so we could provide you with the most efficient services imaginable.

Our professional and committed staff and personnel are always ready to assist you whenever you contact us. So drop us an email or simply call or visit our offices and this could be the beginning of a positive change in your life!

We look forward to being of ultimate assistance to you our dear prospective clients. For more information with regards to our offered products and services, please email us, mbokodopublishers@gmail.com

We look forward to hearing from you soon. God bless you!

Regards,

Publisher